The Wit and Wisdom of
Albert Schweitzer

THE BEACON PRESS
SCHWEITZER SERIES

The Psychiatric Study of Jesus, translated by Charles R. Joy

Albert Schweitzer: An Anthology, edited by Charles R. Joy (published with Harper and Brothers)

The Africa of Albert Schweitzer, by Charles R. Joy and Melvin Arnold (published with Harper and Brothers)

Albert Schweitzer: Life and Message, by Magnus Ratter

Goethe: Four Studies by Albert Schweitzer, translated, with an introduction, by Charles R. Joy

The Wit and Wisdom of Albert Schweitzer, edited by Charles R. Joy

IN PREPARATION

The Animal World of Albert Schweitzer, translated and edited by Charles R. Joy

A Jungle Chronicle, edited by Charles R. Joy

The Wit and Wisdom of Albert Schweitzer

Edited, with an Introduction, by

CHARLES R. JOY

BOSTON · *The Beacon Press* · 1949

First printing, September, 1949
Second printing, October, 1949

Printed in U. S. A.

CONTENTS

ACKNOWLEDGMENTS

Grateful acknowledgment is made to these publishers for their kind permission to reprint copyrighted material from the following books and periodicals:

A. C. Black, Ltd., London, and The Macmillan Company, New York, for excerpts from *The Decay and Restoration of Civilization* (Part I of *The Philosophy of Civilization*), *Civilization and Ethics* (Part II of *The Philosophy of Civilization*), *J. S. Bach*, *On the Edge of the Primeval Forest*, *Paul and His Interpreters*, and *The Quest of the Historical Jesus.*

Christendom, New York, for excerpts from "The Ethics of Reverence for Life" (Vol. I, No. 2).

The Christian Century, Chicago, for excerpts from "Religion and Modern Civilization" (Vol. LI, Nos. 47 and 48).

Dodd, Mead Company, New York, for excerpts from *The Mystery of the Kingdom of God.*

George Allen & Unwin, Ltd., London, and Henry Holt and Company, New York, for excerpts from *Christianity and the Religions of the World.*

George Allen & Unwin, Ltd., and The Macmillan Company, New York, for excerpts from *Memoirs of Childhood and Youth.*

Henry Holt and Company, New York, for excerpts from *The Forest Hospital at Lambarêné*, *Indian Thought and Its Development*, *The Mysticism of Paul the Apostle*, and *Out of My Life and Thought.*

The Wit and Wisdom of
Albert Schweitzer

Introduction

"An aphorism is the last link in a long chain of thought," said Marie von Ebner-Eschenbach, the Viennese writer. In this book we have a collection of the aphorisms of one of the world's consecrated thinkers. They have been piled together —these sayings, and maxims, and apothegms, these incisive comments upon the great problems of life and destiny—in fifteen little gleaming heaps. Yet each little heap, despite its certain symmetry, is but a collection of isolated links, each of which was originally the last link in a long chain of thought. No one who contents himself with reading these brief sentences and short paragraphs will discover Albert Schweitzer. A reader may, indeed, discover himself, as some profound thought in small compass sends him in quest of that most significant and elusive reality which is his own spirit; but if he would find Albert Schweitzer, then he must turn to other books containing the long chains of thought from which these last, lovely links are detached.

One hesitates to subject Albert Schweitzer's books to the process of winnowing or sifting necessary to make such a choice as the following collection represents. We are not dealing here with wheat and chaff. We are not picking out the nuggets of gold left when our placer mining has washed the gravel away. To take these last links from the chains to which they belong is to do violence to the whole.

One hesitates, indeed, to speak of aphorisms and apothegms, for the words seem to imply some over-conscious artistry, some subtle word craftsmanship, some stylistic preoccupation. Here are aphorisms, but Albert Schweitzer is no aphorist; here are apothegms, but Albert Schweitzer is no apothegmatist; here are sentences of rare beauty, but Albert Schweitzer is no sententious stylist. We have here to do with a man who has but one concern—the truth; who believes that truth must be attained through thought, and that thought must be expressed in clear and simple words. If we find here no chiseled cameos of perfect beauty, it is because truth has a loveliness that needs no chiseling. It needs only to be found and described in language that is crystal-clear.

Erckmann, the great Alsatian dramatist, gave this counsel to writers: "First of all write only for yourself. One does nothing well, if while he writes he asks, 'Will this please someone or displease someone else.' The only thing that matters is to please oneself. And not even that. One must say what one has in his own heart to say, just for his heart's satisfaction." Schweitzer, who is Erckmann's fellow countryman, exemplifies this counsel. He has written only what he found in his heart to say.

If it were not that these last links of thought are found in books that the ordinary man never reads—books on New Testament criticism, musical interpretation, philosophical abstractions, theological theories, and Eastern mysticism—we might leave them where they are, for men to discover and comprehend. As it is, we venture to collect these shining, golden links, hoping that they may form in the reader's mind a new and precious synthesis, even though it be not the synthesis from which they came.

Schweitzer made one effort at prosody and gave it up. He once attempted to paint and never made a second effort. Yet there is something of the poet and much of the painter in him. This is, indeed, consistent with his own theory of art. "Art in itself is neither painting nor poetry nor music, but an act of creation in which all three co-operate," he says.[1] "The artist is not only a painter, or only a poet, or only a musician, but all in one. Various artists have their habitation in his soul." [2] Certainly, in Schweitzer's soul, various artists have their habitation. Music is at the very core of his life, for he might have made music his profession; as it is, he has attained rare eminence in it. His prose is full of poetry—the natural, instinctive poetry of a man who is trying to create beauty and to live his life like a song. His thoughts fall inevitably into pictorial shape. Schweitzer: theologian, philosopher, musician, teacher, physician, poet, painter, spiritual pioneer, the servant of the servants of men—what a company of artists is here!

How easily and simply his thoughts take the form of pictures! "Mysticism," he says, "is not the blossom itself, but only the green calyx which is its support. The blossom

[1] *Bach*, II, 13.

[2] *Ibid.*, p. 8.

is ethics."[3] "Only an infinitesimal part of infinite being can ever be affected by my personality. All the rest floats past me utterly indifferent to my existence, like far-away ships to which I make futile signals."[4] "No ray of sunlight is ever lost, but the green which it wakes into existence needs time to sprout, and it is not always granted to the sower to live to see the harvest."[5] "The enthusiasm that comes from thought has the same relation to that which is produced by mere random feeling as the wind which sweeps the heights has to that which eddies about between the hills."[6]

So Schweitzer's mind works. It has been enriched, of course, by the most extraordinary breadth of experience. He studied in three different countries and became a master in four different spheres of learning; he has traveled in a dozen different lands and knows two continents intimately. He has been a teacher of the cultured and learned and wealthy; he has sat at the feet of the primitive and ignorant and impoverished. In the highest circles, as in the lowest, he has been at ease. Lecturing in the great universities of Europe, and preaching his parables of truth to native audiences who can understand only the simplest ethical lessons; playing the organ in great churches, and his tropical piano in primeval jungles; relieving the pain in a broken human body, and gently lifting a toad out of the posthole into which it has fallen—he has been the same under all circumstances: a delicately tuned, wonderfully responsive, simple and

[3] *Ethics*, p. 247. [4] *Ibid.*, p. 249. [5] *Childhood*, p. 102. [6] *Decay*, p. 88.

humble benefactor of mankind.

It was a favored household into which Albert Schweitzer was born on January 14, 1875, a home not of wealth, but of culture and affection. His father was a pastor at Kaysersberg, and his mother the daughter of another preacher in the same Alsatian countryside. Back of his father were teachers and musicians. Albert spent a sheltered and fairly happy childhood at Gunsbach to which the family early moved, although for a time his father was troubled with much sickness. It was a home of simple piety, of devotion to high ideals. It was also a home of music, and even at the age of five Albert was having lessons from his father on the old inherited square piano.

Later, when Albert looked back upon these tender years, he questioned whether he had ever known a perfectly carefree moment then. The reason was that he was an unusually sensitive child, almost abnormally so, and he was made profoundly unhappy by the poverty, sickness, and pain he saw around him; even the suffering of animals disturbed him deeply. And there were sometimes moments of tension at home when he refused to enjoy the special privileges and favors showered upon him as the village pastor's son. He did not care to wear clothes or shoes or hats that the humbler boys in the village did not possess.

Very early in his life, the full significance of the parable of Dives and Lazarus was borne in upon him. There were the people with place and honor and fortune and ease on the one side, and there were the abandoned children, the beaten animals, the starving poor, the suffering sick on the other. Dives with his rich banquets, Lazarus with his open sores. There in that lovely district of rounded hills and fertile valleys and nestling villages, the convictions of his life began to form, and the direction of his life to be fixed. Later it was the Lazarus of Africa that called insistently to him for succor—to him, the Dives of Europe.

Up to the age of thirty his education took the form that might have been anticipated for an evangelical minister's brilliant son whose mind and heart had been richly endowed at birth: the village school, the *Realschule* where modern languages were taught, the *Gymnasium* where a classical education was given, and finally the theological seminary at the University of Strassburg. He was not always a brilliant scholar. Mathematics and languages came hard to him, history and natural science interested him. In composition he was usually first in his class.

The square piano gave way to the organ, his first instructor being Eugène Munch, the young organist at St. Stephen's in Mulhouse, who introduced him to the music of Johann Sebastian Bach. Munch, who died in the full promise of his youth, was ever after affectionately remembered by Albert Schweitzer. His second instructor was the famous organ master of St. Sulpice in Paris, Charles Marie Widor. It is difficult to say which of the two gained more from their happy and fruitful co-operation. From Widor, Schweitzer learned the significance of the architectonic in music; from Schweitzer, Widor learned how to interpret the music of

Bach. Out of their collaboration came, later, Schweitzer's monumental two-volume work on Bach, in which he not only outlined the life of the great cantor of St. Thomas, but also analyzed and interpreted his musical creations.

Thus early in his youth an artistic career opened to Albert Schweitzer. This led to a doctorate in music, recognized eminence as one of the world's great organists and as an authority on the art of organ building, and an undisputed reputation as a great authority on the music of Bach. Here was success enough to satisfy the most ambitious of men.

Schweitzer, however, was no ambitious self-seeker. He cared nothing for fame. He sought only to give expression to what was in him, to seek the ultimate truth of life and the universe, so far as he could discover it. At the university he plunged immediately into philosophical and theological disciplines. His questing, restless, eager mind was not satisfied with accepted interpretations. One day during his year of compulsory military training he was reading in Greek the tenth and eleventh chapters of the book of Matthew, and what he found there started a chain of thought that led to some of the most brilliant books of his career, books on Jesus and Paul, the Last Supper and the Baptism. These books invalidated the lifework of some of the greatest New Testament scholars of his time, and destroyed once and for all the late nineteenth-century conception of Jesus that had been developed by liberal Protestantism.

Schweitzer showed conclusively that Jesus was the child of his age, that he shared the eschatological ideas of late

Judaism, that he looked for an immediate end of the world, that he believed he was to be the Messiah and rule in the new Kingdom of God when the end came. At first Jesus thought the Messianic reign would begin before the disciples had returned from the teaching mission on which he had sent them. Then, when he found that he had been mistaken, he arrived at the conclusion that he must suffer an atoning sacrifice, and that on the cross the great transformation would come. This, too, failed to happen, and so the despairing cry: "My God, my God, why hast thou forsaken me?"

With these books the ideas about Jesus with which many of us were brought up became forever impossible. Said Schweitzer: "The Jesus of Nazareth who came forward publicly as the Messiah, who preached the ethic of the Kingdom of God, who founded the kingdom of Heaven upon earth, and died to give his work its final consecration, never had any existence. He is a figure designed by rationalism, endowed with life by liberalism, and clothed by modern theology in an historical garb." [7]

Yet this does not alter the fact that a tremendous spiritual force streamed forth from Jesus of Nazareth and flows through our own age—a fact that historical research cannot undermine, a fact that is the foundation of all Christianity. "In reality," wrote Schweitzer, "that which is eternal in the words of Jesus is due to the very fact that they are based on an eschatological world-view, and contain the expression of a mind for which the contemporary world

[7] *Quest*, p. 396.

with its historical and social circumstances no longer had any existence. They are appropriate, therefore, to any world, for in every world they raise the man who dares to meet their challenge, and does not turn and twist them into meaninglessness, above his world and his time, making him inwardly free, so that he is fitted to be, in his own world and in his own time, a simple channel of the power of Jesus." [8]

Inevitably Schweitzer's theological studies led to the degree of Doctor of Theology, his appointment to the staff of the Theological Seminary at Strassburg, and his acceptance of a call to serve as a pastor at St. Nicholas in the same city. Preaching became, he said, an inner necessity of his being.

His doctoral degree in philosophy, however, preceded his doctorate in theology. For this degree he prepared a memorable thesis on *The Religious Philosophy of Kant from "The Critique of Pure Reason" to "Religion within the Bounds of Mere Reason,"* in which, by an analysis of the variant meanings of the words that Kant used, he showed that Kant's philosophy was in a constant state of flux. Kant's religious philosophy loses its logical consistency as it gains in profundity.

Schweitzer's interest in philosophy, thus early manifested, has continued to his later life. It found expression, in the midst of many other demands, in a book on *Indian Thought and Its Development* and, most significantly, in his climactic work on *The Philosophy of Civilization.* The

---

[8] *Ibid.*, p. 400.

latter work, as Schweitzer planned it, fell into four great sections: (1) a description of the decay of civilization and its causes, (2) a discussion of the ethical foundations of civilization, (3) an exposition of the world-view of Reverence for Life, and (4) a study of the civilized state. Upon this work Schweitzer has been occupied for almost half a century. He began to write it in 1900; it is now at last reaching its final stages. The book has ripened in the quiet of the primeval forest, but the intermittent work on it has been carried on everywhere as opportunity permitted.

Schweitzer had come to feel that the aesthetic, historical, and material factors do not constitute the essence of civilization. The inner nature of civilization is ultimately ethical. According to Schweitzer, civilization begins when men determine to give themselves with enthusiasm and self-sacrifice to the progressive service of life and the world. This, of course, is a moral conception of civilization that is completely new in the thinking of our age.

For some time Schweitzer was baffled in his effort to answer the profound question: "Is it at all possible to find a real and permanent foundation in thought for a theory of the universe which shall be both ethical and affirmative of the world and of life?" The answer came in a flash of mystic illumination. Schweitzer was making a long and slow journey in a little steamer towing an overladen barge up an African river. He was the only white man on board. As the steamer felt its way laboriously and tediously among the sandbanks of the stream, Schweitzer sat covering paper after paper with disconnected sentences, trying to keep his mind focused on the problem, for which he had found no answer in any philosophy.

Late in the third day of his journey, he tells us, "at the very moment when, at sunset, we were making our way through a herd of hippopotamuses, there flashed upon my mind, unforeseen and unsought, the phrase, 'Reverence for Life.' The iron door had yielded: the path in the thicket had become visible. Now I had found my way to the idea in which world- and life-affirmation and ethics are contained side by side! Now I knew that the world-view of ethical world- and life-affirmation, together with its ideals of civilization, is founded in thought." [9] So was kindled the light which has since made clear every path his thought has traveled.

The most immediate fact in human consciousness is the realization: "I am life which wills to live, in the midst of life which wills to live." [10] I must, therefore, revere my own life and the life around me. "A man is ethical," said Schweitzer, "only when life, as such, is sacred to him, that of plants and animals as that of his fellowmen, and when he devotes himself helpfully to all life that is in need of help." [11] Ethics are absolutely boundless in their domain and in their demands. This is the ethical foundation of Schweitzer's philosophy of civilization. The ultimate source of all the catastrophes and misery of our times is the lack of any consistent ethical theory of the universe. When we begin to work

[9] *Life*, p. 185f. [10] *Ibid.*, p. 186. [11] *Ibid.*, p. 188.

together for a theory of the universe and life, when we begin to give ourselves to our own spiritual and ethical self-fulfillment and to the task of helping forward such spiritual and ethical self-fulfillment in all other life around us, we shall become civilized men and shall save this civilization that totters on the brink of ruin and despair.

So Schweitzer developed as a musician, as a theologian, as a philosopher, carrying on these three separate careers simultaneously, throughout his fruitful life. There was, however, a fourth career, that of healing. One bright sunlit morning at Gunsbach, during the Whitsuntide holidays of 1896, when he was only twenty-one years old, he set the course of his life in quiet deliberation. He determined that he would live for science and art until he was thirty and then devote himself to the immediate service of suffering humanity.

On October 13, 1905, he dropped letters into a mailbox on the Avenue de la Grande Armée in Paris, informing his parents and friends that at the beginning of the winter term he would enter himself as a medical student in order to go to French Equatorial Africa as a doctor. He was fulfilling the promise he had made to himself, for he was then thirty years old.

On the afternoon of Good Friday, 1913, while the bells were ringing from the steeple of the church, Schweitzer and his wife left the old home at Gunsbach for Lambarene in French Equatorial Africa to begin his work at the station of the Paris Missionary Society. He had raised all the money for his hospital himself so as not to be a financial burden to the Society; he had agreed not to preach so as not to be a theological burden to them. His services as a physician were welcome, his orthodoxy was in bad repute.

The work began in an old chicken house which was his first consulting room. The next autumn a small corrugated-iron building with a palm-tile roof was added. Gradually bamboo huts for the patients and other buildings for general purposes sprang up around the central one. By waterways in dugouts the patients came, until at the end of a few months accommodations had to be found for forty patients every day. Quickly the new physician won the respect of the natives and missionaries alike. Finally he was even invited to preach and so was released from his promise in Paris, "*d'être muet comme une carpe.*"

Two years passed. The Schweitzers were preparing to return to Europe for a season of refreshment when, on August 5, 1914, the news of the outbreak of war arrived. The French authorities immediately stopped the work of the hospital and interned the Alsatians in the mission house. In September, 1917, the Schweitzers were transferred to Europe as prisoners of war, and interned in camps at Garaison in the Pyrenees, and later at Saint Rémy in Provence, in the very monastery where Vincent Van Gogh had spent unhappy months as a sufferer from mental disease. Finally they were exchanged for other prisoners and went back to Alsace. Here in the Gunsbach of his early days Schweitzer re-established himself, writing, preaching, lecturing, and playing the organ. After the war he traveled to many parts of Europe to bring his art and his thought to audiences eager to hear him.

It was not until almost ten years after the sudden interruption of his work in Africa that he was at last able to return again to the task so rudely halted. At sunrise on April 19, 1924 (it was Easter eve), Schweitzer found himself again in Lambarene. There was little left of the hospital. All but the small building of corrugated iron and the hardwood frame of one of the bamboo huts had disappeared. For months the man who was a doctor in the mornings had to become a master builder in the afternoons, and it was not until the fall of 1925 that the hospital was rebuilt. Two new doctors and two new nurses had come out to help him. Then came an emergency that brought about a radical change. The exploitation of the forest by the natives had caused them to neglect their little plantations, and a terrible famine began. This was accompanied by a severe epidemic of dysentery. The need of larger facilities became evident. It was impossible for the hospital to spread out. On all sides it was shut in by water, swamp, and hill. It was impossible to prevent infection of the entire hospital by isolating the dysentery patients. There was no way of taking adequate care of the mental patients. It was evident that the hospital would have to move.

It was with a heavy heart that the decision was made to shift the hospital three kilometers up the river to a better, roomier site. Then for a year and a half all medical work was turned over to his colleagues while Schweitzer himself gave all his time to clearing the site for buildings and gardens, and to erecting the desperately needed structures. Most of the work had to be done by native volunteers who would not work for anyone but the "old" doctor. In January, 1927, some of the buildings were ready and the transfer of patients began. By the middle of the summer the new institution could accommodate two hundred patients.

Another two years in Europe, writing, speaking, playing the organ—then a third return to Africa. More building to be done! It seemed as if the demands would never cease to grow. But by this time the hospital had won the confidence of men and women for hundreds of miles around. People who had spent weeks on the journey came for operations. Sufficient supplies arrived for the work. The gardens bore fruit. The deep resolve taken long before on that bright morning in 1896 had produced a magnificent institution of mercy. Between the water and the jungle the hospital was firmly rooted.

Dr. Schweitzer's withdrawal from the successes of his early life in Europe was in no sense a retreat from the harsh realities of life, and yet it is symbolic of his complete disagreement with the spirit of the age. For this is an age that has given up thinking, and Schweitzer believes that only by thought can it be rescued. Thought is just as possible in the jungles of the equator as it is in the universities of Europe—perhaps more possible—and the realities of life there are, beyond any question, harsher. Schweitzer, convinced that the world is mysteriously full of suffering, and that he lives in an age of frightful spiritual decadence, is trying by his thinking and by his life to rekindle the fire of thought, and to set in motion new processes of spiritual salvation. In men like him our hope for the future lies.

The pages that follow bring to us a few rays from the many facets of a shining life.

CHARLES R. JOY

The Wit and Wisdom of
Albert Schweitzer

KEY TO THE ABBREVIATIONS

Bach	*J. S. Bach.* New York: The Macmillan Company, 1938.
Childhood	*Memoirs of Childhood and Youth.* New York: The Macmillan Company, 1931.
Christianity	*Christianity and the Religions of the World.* New York: Henry Holt and Company, 1939.
Decay	*The Decay and Restoration of Civilization* (Part I of *The Philosophy of Civilization*). New York: The Macmillan Company, 1932.
Edge	*On the Edge of the Primeval Forest.* New York: The Macmillan Company, 1931.
Ethics	*Civilization and Ethics* (Part II of *The Philosophy of Civilization*). New York: The Macmillan Company, 1929.
Goethe	*Goethe: Four Studies.* Boston: The Beacon Press, 1949.
Hospital	*The Forest Hospital at Lambaréné.* New York: Henry Holt and Company, 1931.
Indian	*Indian Thought and Its Development.* New York: Henry Holt and Company, 1936.
Life	*Out of My Life and Thought.* New York: Henry Holt and Company, 1933.
Mystery	*The Mystery of the Kingdom of God.* New York: Dodd, Mead and Company, 1914.
Mysticism	*The Mysticism of Paul the Apostle.* New York: Henry Holt and Company, 1931.
Paul	*Paul and His Interpreters.* New York: The Macmillan Company, 1912.
Quest	*The Quest of the Historical Jesus.* New York: The Macmillan Company, 1926.
Religion	"Religion and Modern Civilization." Chicago: *The Christian Century*, LI (1934), 1483–84, 1519–21.
Reverence	"The Ethics of Reverence for Life." New York: *Christendom*, I (1936), 225–39.

Thought

Thought becomes religious when it thinks itself out to the end. [Ethics, p. 258]

We must all become religious as the result of reflection. [Ethics, p. xviii]

We must all venture once more to become "thinkers," in order to attain to that mysticism which is the only immediate and the only profound world-view.

[Ethics, p. xviii]

We must all make pilgrimage through the realm of knowledge until we reach the point where it passes into actual experience of the world's essential being.

[Ethics, p. xviii]

It has a significance for all future times that the Symphony of Christianity began with a tremendous dissonance between faith and thought, which later resolved itself into a harmony. [Mysticism, p. 377]

I was convinced—and I am so still—that the fundamental principles of Christianity have to be proved true by reasoning, and by no other method.

[Childhood, p. 60]

If thought is to set out on its journey unhampered, it must be prepared for anything, even for arrival at intellectual agnosticism. [Decay, p. 104]

Faith has nothing to fear from thinking, even when the latter disturbs its peace and raises a debate which appears to promise no good results for the religious life. [Mysticism, p. 376]

The first active deed of thinking is resignation—acquiescence in what happens. [Religion, p. 1520]

The spirit of the age dislikes what is simple. It no longer believes the simple can be profound. It loves the complicated, and regards it as profound.

[Religion, p. 1484]

The spirit of the age loves dissonance, in tones, in lines and in thought. That shows how far from thinking it is, for thinking is a harmony within us.

[Religion, p. 1484]

Karl Barth, who is the most modern theologian, because he lives most in the spirit of our age, more than any other has that contempt for thinking which is characteristic of our age. [Religion, p. 1484]

Dogmatic religion is based on the creeds, the early church and the reformation. It has no relations with thinking, but emphasizes the difference between thinking and believing. [Religion, p. 1484]

In modern thinking the same thing happens as in religion. Thinking drops the tiller from its hand in the middle of the storm. [Religion, p. 1520]

If the debate between tradition and thought falls silent, Christian truth suffers, and with it Christian intellectual integrity. [Mysticism, p. 377]

It will ever remain incomprehensible that our generation, which has shown itself so great by its achievements in discovery and invention, could fall so low spiritually as to give up thinking. [Life, p. 257]

Renunciation of thinking is a declaration of spiritual bankruptcy. [Life, p. 258]

With its depreciation of thinking our generation has lost its feeling for sincerity and with it that for truth as well. [Life, p. 260]

Christianity has need of thought that it may come to the consciousness of its real self. For centuries it treasured the great commandment of love and mercy as traditional truth without recognizing it as a reason for opposing slavery, witch-burning, torture, and all the other ancient and medieval forms of inhumanity. [Life, p. 275]

We are like springs of water which no longer run because they have not been watched and have gradually become choked with rubbish. [Decay, p. 92f.]

More than any other age has our own neglected to watch the thousand springs of thought; hence the drought in which we are pining. But if we only go on to remove the rubbish which conceals the water, the sands will be irrigated again, and life will spring up where hitherto there has been only a desert. [Decay, p. 93]

How . . . true it is that the injustice and violence and untruth, which are now bringing so much disaster on the human race, would lose their power if only a single real trace of reflection about the meaning of the world and of life should appear amongst us! [Decay, p. 103]

The conviction that in after life we must struggle to remain thinking as freely and feeling as deeply as we did in our youth, has accompanied me on my road through life as a faithful advisor. [Childhood, p. 97]

To be truly rational is to become ethical.
[Reverence, p. 231]

Whatever is reasonable is good.
[Reverence, p. 231]

All real progress in the world is in the last analysis produced by rationalism. [Decay, p. 89]

Reason is given us that we may bring everything within the range of its action, even the most exalted ideas of religion. [Childhood, p. 60]

"The negroes are deeper than we are," a white man once said to me, "because they don't read newspapers," and the paradox has some truth in it.
[Edge, p. 154]

Only when thinking becomes quite humble can it set its feet upon the way that leads to knowledge.
[Religion, p. 1520]

The deepest thinking is humble. It is only concerned that the flame of truth which it keeps alive should burn with the strongest and purest heat; it does not trouble about the distance to which its brightness penetrates.

[Indian, p. 257]

Facts call us to reflect, even as the tossings of a capsizing vessel cause the crew to rush on deck and to climb the masts. [Ethics, p. 286]

All thinking is strengthened by the fact that in any given moment it must find its way through reality and no longer concern itself with imagined things.

[Goethe, p. 110]

Thinking which keeps contact with reality must look up to the heavens, it must look over the earth, and dare to direct its gaze to the barred windows of a lunatic asylum. [Religion, p. 1520]

The enthusiasm which comes from thought has the same relation to that which is produced by mere random feeling as the wind which sweeps the heights has to that which eddies about between the hills. [Decay, p. 88]

When in the spring the withered grey of the pastures gives place to green, this is due to the millions of young shoots which sprout up freshly from the old roots. In like manner the revival of thought which is essential for our time can only come through a transformation of the opinions and ideals of the many brought about by individual and universal reflection about the meaning of life and of the world. [Decay, p. 101]

Just as a tree bears year after year the same fruit and yet fruit which is each year new, so must all permanently valuable ideas be continually born again in thought. [Life, p. 259]

It is from new ideas that we must build history anew. [Decay, p. 86]

Truth

Let us rejoice in the Truth, wherever we find its lamp burning. [Christianity, p. 51]

Truth has no special time of its own. Its hour is now—always, and indeed then most truly when it seems most unsuitable to actual circumstances.
[Edge, p. 174]

Only an age which can show the courage of sincerity can possess truth which works as a spiritual force within it. [Life, p. 260]

An idea is, in the end, always stronger than circumstances. [Bach, I, p. 36]

Behind Success comes Truth, and her reward is with her. [Quest, p. 12]

The city of truth cannot be built on the swampy ground of skepticism. [Life, p. 259]

Our age is bent on trying to make the barren tree of skepticism fruitful by tying fruits of truth on its branches. [Life, p. 259]

Those who work to make our age skeptical . . . do so in the expectation that, as a result of renouncing all hope of self-discovered truth, men will end by accepting as truth what is forced upon them with authority and by propaganda. [Life, p. 258]

The theory of double truth is a spiritual danger. If there is a double truth, there is no truth.

[Religion, p. 1520]

It is through the idealism of youth that man catches sight of truth, and in that idealism he possesses a wealth which he must never exchange for anything else.

[Childhood, p. 99]

For us the great men are not those who solved the problems, but those who discovered them.

[Quest, p. 159]

If the talents succumb to the errors of their time, what matters? But when the men of genius are ensnared in them, centuries have to suffer for it.

[Bach, I, p. 96]

He [Hegel] wrote: "What is reasonable is real, and what is real is reasonable." On the night of June 25, 1820, when that sentence was written, our age began, the age which moved on to the world war—and which perhaps some day will end civilization! [Religion, p. 1483]

The result of the voyage does not depend on the speed of the ship, whether it be a fast sailer or somewhat slower, nor on the method of propulsion, whether by sails or by steam, but on whether or not it keeps a true course and whether or not its steering-gear remains in order.

[Ethics, p. 3]

Must we either drift aimlessly through lack of reflection or sink in pessimism as the result of reflection? No. We must indeed attempt the limitless ocean, but we may set our sails and steer a determined course.

[Ethics, p. 220f.]

The pathway from imperfect to perfect recognized truth leads through the valley of reality. European thought has already descended into this valley. Indian thought is still on the hill on this side of it. If it wishes to climb to the hill beyond, it must first go down into the valley. [Indian, p. 256f.]

There are some who are historians by the grace of God, who from their mother's womb have an instinctive feeling for the real. They follow through all the intricacy and confusion of reported fact the pathway of reality, like a stream which, despite the rocks that encumber its course and the windings of its valley, finds its way inevitably to the sea. [Quest, p. 25]

The highest honor one can show to a system of thought is to test it ruthlessly with a view to discovering how much truth it contains, just as steel is assayed to try its strength. [Indian, p. viii]

The fact is that in theology the most revolutionary ideas are swallowed quite readily so long as they smooth their passage by a few small concessions. It is only when a spicule of bone stands out obstinately and causes. choking that theology begins to take note of dangerous ideas

[Quest, p. 37]

The Little-Faiths will never succeed in suppressing loyalty to truth. [Mysticism, p. 377]

Beauty

In no other art does the perfect consign the imperfect to oblivion so thoroughly as it does in music.

[Bach, I, p. 49]

Art in itself is neither painting nor poetry nor music, but an act of creation in which all three cooperate.

[Bach, II, p. 13]

The artist is not only a painter, or only a poet, or only a musician, but all in one. Various artists have their habitation in his soul. [Bach, II, p. 8]

Painting is suffused with poetry, and poetry with painting. The quality of either of the arts at a given moment depends on the strength or the weakness of this inter-coloration. [Bach, II, p. 11]

Many a man erroneously thinks he sees a picture whereas he really hears it, his artistic emotions arising from the music—perhaps silent—that he perceives in the scene represented on the canvas. Anyone who does not hear the bees in Didier-Pouget's picture of the flowery heath does not see it with the eye of the artist.

[Bach, II, p. 14]

The tragedy of music is it can only express with limited intelligibility the concrete image from which it has sprung. [Bach, II, p. 18]

Bach, like every lofty religious mind, belongs not to the church but to religious humanity, and . . . any room becomes a church in which his sacred works are performed and listened to with devotion. [Bach, I, p. 264]

Whereas at other times and in other places the great artist has been only one star among others, whose light, if less brilliant than his, he nevertheless did not extinguish, Bach is surrounded by mere will-of-the-wisps, which his epoch—and he with it—mistook for stars.

[Bach, I, p. 95f.]

Bach's music is Gothic. Just as in Gothic architecture the great plan develops out of the simple motive, but enfolds itself in the richest detail instead of in rigid line, and only makes its effect when every detail is truly vital, so does the impression a Bach work makes on the hearer depend on the player communicating to him the massive outline and the details together, both equally clear and equally full of life. [Bach, I, p. 363]

Joy, sorrow, tears, lamentation, laughter—to all these it [*The Well-Tempered Clavichord*] gives voice, but in such a way that we are transported from the world of unrest to a world of peace, and see reality in a new way, as if we were sitting by a mountain lake and contemplating hills and woods and clouds in the tranquil and fathomless water.

[Bach, I, p. 338f.]

The Brandenburg concertos are the purest product of Bach's polyphonic style. . . . We really seem to see before us what the philosophy of all ages conceives as the fundamental mystery of things,—that self-unfolding of the idea in which it creates its own opposite in order to overcome it, creates another, which again it overcomes, and so on and on until it finally returns to itself, having meanwhile traversed the whole of existence. [Bach, I, p. 406f.]

Like all music, the figured bass should have no other end and aim than the glory of God and the recreation of the soul; where this is not kept in mind there is no true music, but only an infernal clamor and ranting.

[Bach, I, p. 167]

It happens . . . with the sacred poem as with the lyric: in one inspired song the poet, become for the moment a genius, will express magically what in other songs he could only stammer out. And this one song will live.

[Bach, I, p. 11]

In art, as in everything else, is not all unfolding and ripening a kind of withering, since in the full bloom we no longer have truth and reality appealing to us with that mysterious directness that is more magically eloquent than even perfection itself? [Bach, I, p. 67]

Jesus

In proportion as we have the Spirit of Jesus we have the true knowledge of Jesus. [Quest, p. 399]

There came a Man to rule over the world; He ruled it for good and for ill, as history testifies; He destroyed the world into which He was born; the spiritual life of our own time seems like to perish at His hands, for he leads to battle against our thought a host of dead ideas, a ghostly army upon which death has no power, and Himself destroys again the truth and goodness which His Spirit creates in us, so that it cannot rule the world. That He continues, notwithstanding, to reign as the alone Great and alone True in a world of which He denied the continuance, is the prime example of that antithesis between spiritual and natural truth which underlies all life and all events, and in Him emerges into the field of history. [Quest, p. 2]

In religion there are two different currents: one free from dogma and one that is dogmatic. That which is free from dogma bases itself on the preaching of Jesus; the dogmatic bases itself on the creeds of the early church and the reformation. [Religion, p. 1484]

It was not only each epoch that found its reflection in Jesus; each individual created Him in accordance with his own character. [Quest, p. 4]

We can, at the present day, scarcely imagine the long agony in which the historical view of the life of Jesus came to birth. And even when He was once more recalled to life, He was still, like Lazarus of old, bound hand and foot with grave-clothes—the grave-clothes of dogma.

[Quest, p. 4]

Hate as well as love can write a Life of Jesus, and the greatest of them are written with hate. . . . It was not so much hate of the Person of Jesus as of the supernatural nimbus with which it was so easy to surround Him, and with which He had in fact been surrounded.

[Quest, p. 4]

There is no historical task which so reveals a man's true self as the writing of a Life of Jesus.

[Quest, p. 4]

As of old Jacob wrestled with the angel, so German theology wrestles with Jesus of Nazareth and will not let Him go until He bless it—that is, until He will consent to serve it and will suffer Himself to be drawn by the Germanic spirit into the midst of our time and our civilization. But when the day breaks, the wrestler must let Him go. He will not cross the ford with us. [Quest, p. 310]

Jesus as a concrete historical personality remains a stranger to our time, but His spirit, which lies hidden in His words, is known in simplicity, and its influence is direct. [Quest, p. 399]

Jesus of Nazareth will not suffer Himself to be modernized. As an historic figure He refuses to be detached from His own time. He has no answer for the question, "Tell us Thy name in our speech and for our day!"

[Quest, p. 310f.]

It is a good thing that the true historical Jesus should overthrow the modern Jesus, should rise up against the modern spirit and send upon earth, not peace, but a sword. He was not a teacher, not a casuist; He was an imperious ruler. [Quest, p. 401]

The study of the Life of Jesus has had a curious history. It set out in quest of the historical Jesus, believing that when it had found Him it could bring Him straight into our time as a Teacher and Savior. It loosed the bands by which He had been riveted for centuries to the stony rocks of ecclesiastical doctrine, and rejoiced to see life and movement coming into the figure once more, and the historical Jesus advancing, as it seemed, to meet it. But He does not stay; He passes by our time and returns to His own.

[Quest, p. 397]

Jesus returns to His own time, not owing to the application of any historical ingenuity, but by the same inevitable necessity by which the liberated pendulum returns to its original position. [Quest, p. 397]

As a water plant is beautiful so long as it is growing in the water, but once torn from its roots, withers and becomes unrecognizable, so it is with the historical Jesus when He is wrenched loose from the soil of eschatology, and the attempt is made to conceive Him "historically" as a Being not subject to temporal conditions. [Quest, p. 399]

The Jesus of Nazareth who came forward publicly as the Messiah, who preached the ethic of the Kingdom of God, who founded the Kingdom of Heaven upon earth, and died to give His work its final consecration, never had any existence. He is a figure designed by rationalism, endowed with life by liberalism, and clothed by modern theology in an historical garb. [Quest, p. 396]

The truth is it is not Jesus as historically known, but Jesus as spiritually arisen within men, who is significant for our time and can help it. Not the historical Jesus, but the spirit which goes forth from Him and in the spirits of men strives for new influence and rule, is that which overcomes the world. [Quest, p. 399]

Jesus means something to our world because a mighty spiritual force streams forth from Him and flows through our time also. This fact can neither be shaken nor confirmed by any historical discovery. It is the solid foundation of Christianity. [Quest, p. 397]

We must go back to the point where we can feel again the heroic in Jesus. Before that mysterious Person, who, in the form of his time, knew that he was creating upon the foundation of his life and death a moral world *which bears his name*, we must be forced to lay our faces in the dust, without daring even to wish to understand his nature.

[Mystery, p. 274]

We must take the ethical religion of Jesus out of the setting of his world-view and put it in our own.

[Religion, p. 1484]

The Brahmans and Buddha say to man: "As one who has died, and to whom nothing in the natural world is of interest any longer, you should live in the world of pure spirituality." The gospel of Jesus tells him: "You must become free from the world and from yourself, in order to work in the world as an instrument of God."

[Christianity, p. 37]

Whereas he [Jesus] expected the kingdom of God to come at the end of the world, we must endeavor, under the influence of the spirit of his ethical religion, to make the kingdom of God a reality in this world by works of love. [Religion, p. 1484]

In reality that which is eternal in the words of Jesus is due to the very fact that they are based on an eschatological world-view, and contain the expression of a mind for which the contemporary world with its historical and social circumstances no longer had any existence. They are appropriate, therefore, to any world, for in every world they raise the man who dares to meet their challenge, and does not turn and twist them into meaninglessness, above his world and his time, making him inwardly free, so that he is fitted to be, in his own world and in his own time, a simple channel of the power of Jesus. [Quest, p. 400]

The significance of Jesus for us is that He fights against the spirit of the modern world, forcing it to abandon the low level on which it moves even in its best thoughts and to rise to the height whence we judge things according to the superior will of God, which is active in us, and think no more in terms of human utilitarianism but solely in terms of having to do God's will—becoming forces of God's ethical personality. [Christianity, p. 19f.]

Jesus comes to us as One unknown, without a name, as of old, by the lake-side, He came to those men who knew Him not. He speaks to us the same word: "Follow thou me!" and sets us to the tasks which He has to fulfil for our time. He commands. And to those who obey Him, whether they be wise or simple, He will reveal Himself in the toils, the conflicts, the sufferings which they shall pass through in His fellowship, and, as an ineffable mystery, they shall learn in their own experience Who He Is.

[Quest, p. 401]

Paul

Paul is the patron-saint of thought in Christianity. And all those who think to serve the faith in Jesus by destroying freedom of thought would do well to keep out of his way. [Mysticism, p. 377]

It is the fate of the "Little-Faiths" of truth that they, true followers of Peter, whether they be of the Roman or the Protestant observance, cry out and sink in the sea of ideas, where the followers of Paul, believing in the Spirit, walk secure and undismayed. [Paul, p. 249]

Paul, alone of all the believers of this early period, recognizes that faith in Jesus Christ essentially, and with all that it implies, must place itself under the absolute authority of the ethical, and must draw its warmth from the flame of love. [Mysticism, p. 310]

The ideal of Paul's ethic is to live with the eyes fixed upon eternity, while standing firmly upon the solid ground of reality. [Mysticism, p. 333]

As the spider's net is an admirably simple construction so long as it remains stretched between the threads which hold it in position, but becomes a hopeless tangle as soon as it is loosed from them; so the Pauline Mysticism is an admirably simple thing, so long as it is set in the framework of eschatology, but becomes a hopeless tangle as soon as it is cut loose from this.

[Mysticism, p. 140]

As radium by its very nature is in a constant state of emanation, so Pauline mysticism is constantly being transmuted from the natural to the spiritual and ethical.

[Mysticism, p. 385]

Paul leads us out upon the path of true redemption, and hands us over, prisoners, to Christ.

[Mysticism, p. 396]

Paul is no mere revolutionary. He takes the faith of the Primitive-Christian community as his starting-point: only he will not consent to halt where it comes to an end, but claims the right to think out his thoughts about Christ to their conclusion, without caring whether the truths which he thereby reaches have ever come within the purview of the faith held by the Christian community and been recognized by it. [Mysticism, p. 376]

Christianity

Christianity cannot take the place of thinking, but it must be founded on it. [Life, p. 276]

Just as a stream is preserved from gradually leaking away, because it flows along above subsoil water, so does Christianity need the subsoil water of elemental piety which is the fruit of thinking. [Life, p. 276]

The situation to-day is that Christianity has completely withdrawn into itself, and is concerned only with the propagation of its own ideas, as such. [Life, p. 274]

To make up to itself for the fact that it does so little to prove the reality of its spiritual and ethical nature, the Christianity of today cheats itself with the delusion that it is making its position as a Church stronger year by year. [Life, p. 276]

The essential element in Christianity as it was preached by Jesus and as it is comprehended by thought, is this, that it is only through love that we can attain to communion with God. [Life, p. 277]

Christianity is not consistent. In the bed-rock of its pessimism there are optimistic veins, for it is not only the religion of redemption but of the Kingdom of God. Therefore, it wishes and hopes for a transformation of the world. [Christianity, p. 13]

In its death-pangs eschatology bore to the Greek genius a wonder-child, the mystic, sensuous, Early-Christian doctrine of immortality, and consecrated Christianity as the religion of immortality to take the place of the slowly dying civilization of the ancient world.

[Quest, p. 254]

That which appears to be *naïveté* in Christianity is in reality its profundity. [Christianity, p. 71]

God

All living knowledge of God rests upon this foundation: that we experience Him in our lives as Will-to-Love. [Life, p. 277]

To be glad instruments of God's love in this imperfect world is the service to which men are called, and it forms a preparatory stage to this bliss that awaits them in the perfected world, the Kingdom of God.

[Christianity, p. 14]

As a star, by the inner law of the light which is in it, shines over a dark world, even when there is no prospect of heralding a morning which is to dawn upon it, so the Elect must radiate the light of the Kingdom in the world.

[Mysticism, p. 389]

Christianity shows itself as the religion which, penetrating and transcending all knowledge, reaches forward to the ethical, living God, who cannot be found through contemplation of the world, but reveals Himself in man only. [Christianity, p. 83]

Have no fear of natural science—it brings us nearer to God. [Religion, p. 1520]

I live my life in God, in the mysterious ethical divine personality which I cannot discover in the world, but only experience in myself as a mysterious impulse.

[Ethics, p. xvi]

With the best intentions, we are constantly in danger of giving our allegiance to an externalized Kingdom-of-God belief. [Mysticism, p. 388]

To the question, how a man can be in the world and in God at one and the same time, we find this answer in the Gospel of Jesus: "By living and working in this world as one who is not *of* the world."

[Christianity, p. 71]

There is an ocean—cold water without motion. In this ocean, however, is the Gulf Stream, hot water flowing from the Equator towards the Pole. Inquire of all scientists how it is physically imaginable that a stream of hot water flows between the waters of the ocean, which, so to speak, form its banks, the moving within the motionless, the hot within the cold, no scientist can explain it. Similarly, there is the God of love within the God of the forces of the universe—one with Him, and yet so totally different. We let ourselves be seized and carried away by that vital stream. [Christianity, p. 76]

We, too, like the early Christians, are taught by God the awful discipline of the word: "My thoughts are not your thoughts." He sets before us the difficult task of being faithful to the Kingdom of God as those who do not see and yet believe. [Christianity, p. 80]

We, having lived through, and still living in, a time of appalling and meaningless events, feel as if a terrible tidal wave had flung us back, far away from the harbor of the Kingdom of God, towards which we now have to start out afresh, rowing hard against storm and tide, without being certain of really making headway.

[Christianity, p. 80]

The great weakness of all doctrines of redemption since the primitive Christian is that they represent a man as wholly concerned with his own individual redemption, and not equally with the coming of the Kingdom of God. [Mysticism, p. 384]

All questions of religion tend towards the one which comprises them all: How can I conceive of myself as being in the world and at the same time in God? All the questions of Christian theology, too, in all the centuries, go back to this one. [Christianity, p. 26f.]

It is only through the idea of the Kingdom of God that religion enters into relationship with civilization.

[Religion, p. 1484]

Optimism

Religion is more than negation of life and of the world. [Christianity, p. 45]

I think I am the first Western thinker who has dared to be absolutely skeptical with regard to our knowledge of the objective world, without at the same time renouncing world- and life-affirmation and ethics.

[Ethics, p. xiii]

The higher powers of volition and creation are becoming exhausted because the optimism from which they ought to draw their life-energy has been gradually and unconsciously sapped by the pessimism which has interpenetrated its substance. [Ethics, p. 16]

Our degeneration, when it is traced back to its origin in our view of the world, really consists in the fact that true optimism has vanished unperceived from our midst. [Ethics, p. 16]

We are always walking on loose stones which overhang the precipice of pessimism. [Ethics, p. 224]

The poisonous germs of phthisis induce in the sufferer the so-called *euphory*, that is, a subjective feeling of well-being and of energy. Similarly, a superficial and externalized optimism comes to view amongst the masses of men when individuals and society have been injected with pessimism without being conscious of the fact.

[Ethics, p. 17]

True optimism has no connection whatever with overindulgent judgments of any kind. It consists in conceiving and willing the ideal, as this is inspired by profound and self-consistent affirmation of life and of the world.

[Ethics, p. 17]

To the question whether I am a pessimist or an optimist, I answer that my knowledge is pessimistic, but my willing and hoping are optimistic. [Life, p. 279]

Character

The highest proof of the Spirit is love. Love is the eternal thing which men can already on earth possess as it really is. [Life, p. 249]

Does my behavior in respect of love effect nothing? That is because there is not enough love in me. Am I powerless against the untruthfulness and the lies which have their being all around me? The reason is that I myself am not truthful enough. Have I to watch dislike and ill will carrying on their sad game? That means that I myself have not yet completely laid aside small-mindedness and envy. Is my love of peace misunderstood and scorned? That means that I am not yet sufficiently peace-loving.

[Childhood, p. 101]

Anyone can rescue his human life, in spite of his professional life, who seizes every opportunity of being a man by means of personal action, however unpretending, for the good of fellow-men who need the help of a fellow-man.

[Life, p. 113]

Anyone who proposes to do good must not expect people to roll stones out of his way, but must accept his lot calmly if they even roll a few more upon it.

[Life, p. 112]

All the kindness which a man puts out into the world works on the heart and the thoughts of mankind, but we are so foolishly indifferent that we are never in earnest in the matter of kindness. We want to topple a great load over, and yet will not avail ourselves of a lever which would multiply our power a hundred-fold.

[Childhood, p. 103]

I must forgive the lies directed against myself, because my own life has been so many times blotted by lies; I must forgive the lovelessness, the hatred, the slander, the fraud, the arrogance which I encounter, since I myself have so often lacked love, hated, slandered, defrauded, and been arrogant. [Ethics, p. 260]

I am obliged to exercise unlimited forgiveness because, if I did not forgive, I should be untrue to myself, in that I should thus act as if I were not guilty in the same way as the other has been guilty with regard to me.

[Ethics, p. 260]

The ripeness that our development must aim at is one which makes us simpler, more truthful, purer, more peace-loving, meeker, kinder, more sympathetic. That is the only way in which we are to sober down with age. That is the process in which the soft iron of youthful idealism hardens into the steel of a full-grown idealism which can never be lost. [Childhood, p. 100]

The knowledge of life which we grown-ups have to pass on to the younger generation will not be expressed thus: "Reality will soon give way before your ideals," but "Grow into your ideals, so that life can never rob you of them." If all of us could become what we were at fourteen, what a different place the world would be!

[Childhood, p. 102]

Just as the water of the streams we see is small in amount compared to that which flows underground, so the idealism which becomes visible is small in amount compared with what men and women bear locked in their hearts, unreleased or scarcely released.

[Life, p. 114]

At the present time when violence, clothed n life, dominates the world more cruelly than it ever has before, I still remain convinced that truth, love, peaceableness, meekness, and kindness are the violence which can master all other violence. [Childhood, p. 102]

The world will be theirs as soon as ever a sufficient number of men with purity of heart, with strength, and with perseverance think and live out the thoughts of love and truth, of meekness and peaceableness.

[Childhood, p. 102f.]

We do not have enough inwardness, we are not sufficiently preoccupied with our own spiritual life, we lack quietness; and this not only because in our exacting, busy existence it is difficult to obtain, but because, ignoring its importance, we do not take pains to secure it, being too easily contented with living our lives as unrecollected men who merely aim at being good. [Christianity, p. 43]

Much that has become our own in gentleness, modesty, kindness, willingness to forgive, in veracity, loyalty, resignation under suffering, we owe to people in whom we have seen or experienced these virtues at work, sometimes in a great matter, sometimes in a small. A thought which had become act sprang into us like a spark, and lighted a new flame within us. [Childhood, p. 90]

The mere setting up of lists of virtues and vices is like vamping on the keyboard and calling the ensuing noise music. [Ethics, p. 25]

Imaginative power, determined by ideals, is at work in all that is. The impulse toward perfection is innate in us—beings, as we are, endowed with freedom and capable of reflective purposive action—in such a way that we naturally aspire to raise ourselves and every portion of existence affected by our influence to the highest material and spiritual degree of value. [Ethics, p. 222]

I do not believe that we can put into anyone ideas which are not in him already. As a rule there are in everyone all sorts of good ideas, ready like tinder. But much of this tinder catches fire, or catches it successfully, only when it meets some flame or spark from outside, i.e. from some other person. [Childhood, p. 91]

We wander through life together in a semi-darkness in which none of us can distinguish exactly the features of his neighbor; only from time to time, through some experience that we have of our companion, or through some remark that he passes he stands for a moment close to us, as though illumined by a flash of lightning.

[Childhood, p. 91]

The soul, too, has its clothing of which we must not deprive it, and no one has a right to say to another: "Because we belong to each other as we do, I have a right to know all your thoughts." [Childhood, p. 92]

To analyze others—unless it be to help back to a sound mind someone who is in spiritual or intellectual confusion—is a rude commencement, for there is a modesty of the soul which we must recognize, just as we do that of the body. [Childhood, p. 92]

A man must not try to force his way into the personality of another. [Childhood, p. 92]

Impart as much as you can of your spiritual being to those who are on the road with you, and accept as something precious what comes back to you from them.

[Childhood, p. 92]

We must all beware of reproaching those we love with want of confidence in us if they are not always ready to let us look into all the corners of their hearts. We might almost say that the better we get to know each other, the more mystery we see in each other.

[Childhood, p. 93]

The one essential thing is that we strive to have light in ourselves. Our strivings will be recognized by others, and when people have light in themselves, it will shine out from them. Then we get to know each other as we walk together in the darkness, without needing to pass our hands over each other's faces, or to intrude into each other's hearts. [Childhood, p. 93f.]

No man is ever completely and permanently a stranger to his fellow-man. Man belongs to man. Man has claims on man. [Childhood, p. 95]

There are no heroes of action: only heroes of renunciation and suffering. [Life, p. 111]

In the parable of Jesus, the shepherd saves not merely the soul of the lost sheep but the whole animal. [Life, p. 270]

It is our task to unearth and proclaim once more the indestructible rights of man, rights which afford the individual the utmost possible freedom for his individuality in his own human group; human rights which guarantee protection to his existence and his personal dignity against every alien power to which he may become subject. [Ethics, p. xx]

Through the power which we win over the forces of nature we get also a gruesome kind of power over our fellow human beings. [Ethics, p. 286]

Sincerity is the first ethical quality which appears. [Reverence, p. 230]

Sincerity is the foundation of the spiritual life. [Life, p. 260]

Civilization

Civilization I define in quite general terms as spiritual and material progress in all spheres of activity, accompanied by an ethical development of individuals and of mankind. [Life, p. 232]

Civilization is progress, material and spiritual progress, on the part of individuals as of the mass. [Decay, p. 35]

We may take as the essential element in civilization the ethical perfecting of the individual and of society as well. [Life, p. 176]

Civilization which develops itself on the material, and not in a corresponding degree on the spiritual side, is like a ship with defective steering-gear, which becomes more unsteerable from moment to moment, and so rushes on to catastrophe. [Ethics, p. 2]

The question of how many or how few material conquests we have to record is not the decisive question for civilization. Its fate hangs on the possession or lack of possession, by convictions and dispositions, of power over matters of fact. [Ethics, p. 3]

What is nationalism? It is an ignoble patriotism, exaggerated till it has lost all meaning, which bears the same relation to the noble and healthy kind as the fixed idea of an imbecile does to normal conviction.

[Decay, p. 48]

Hegel dares to say that everything serves progress. The passions of rulers and of peoples—all are the servants of progress. One can only say that Hegel did not know the passions of people as we know them, or he would not have dared to write that! [Religion, p. 1483]

The man of to-day pursues his dark journey in a time of darkness, as one who has no freedom, no mental collectedness, no all-round development, as one who loses himself in an atmosphere of inhumanity, who surrenders his spiritual independence and his moral judgment to the organized society in which he lives, and who finds himself in every direction up against hindrances to the temper of true civilization. [Decay, p. 34]

The terrible truth that with the progress of history and the economic development of the world it is becoming not easier, but harder, to develop true civilization, has never found utterance. [Decay, p. 34]

The collapse of civilization has come about because we left the whole question of ethics to society. [Ethics, p. 275]

Our civilization is doomed because it has developed with much greater vigor materially than it has spiritually. Its equilibrium has been destroyed. [Ethics, p. 2]

It was our technical progress which made it possible for us to kill, as it were, at a distance and to annihilate men in great masses, so that we came to lay aside the ultimate rules of humanity and to be nothing but blind wills, the servants of perfected instruments of slaughter, unable in their annihilating activity to recognize any longer the difference between combatants and non-combatants. [Ethics, p. 5]

In the last resort it is machinery and world commerce which are responsible for the world-war; and the inventions which gave such mighty destructive power into our hands have given such a form of devastation to the war that it has ruined conquered and conquerors together in an inconceivably short space of time. [Ethics, p. 5]

We are not a race weakened and exhausted by luxury whose task is to rouse itself once more, amid the storms of history, to a condition of efficiency and of idealism. On the contrary, we are hindered and embarrassed in our spiritual conflict by the very efficiency which we have attained in most of the realms of direct objective activity.

[Ethics, p. 6]

Faith in the spiritual progress of man and of humanity has already become almost impossible for us. We must force ourselves to it with the courage of desperation.

[Ethics, p. 286]

We must turn together to will the spiritual progress of man and of humanity in mutual accord and to base our hopes on it once more. This is the putting of the helm hard to port which must be accomplished if our vessel is to be brought head to wind again, even now at the last moment. [Ethics, p. 286]

The old-time rabbis used to teach that the kingdom of God would come if only the whole of Israel would really keep a single Sabbath simultaneously!

[Decay, p. 103]

Religion

One truth stands firm. All that happens in world history rests on something spiritual. If the spiritual is strong, it creates world history. If it is weak, it suffers world history. [Religion, p. 1483f.]

All our advances in knowledge and power will prove fatal to us in the end unless we retain control over them by a corresponding advance in our spirituality.

[Ethics, p. 285f.]

The great question which each religion must be asked is, how far it produces permanent and profound incentives to the inward perfecting of personality and to ethical activity. [Christianity, p. 26]

In religion we try to find an answer to the elementary question with which each one of us is newly confronted every morning, namely, what meaning and what value is to be ascribed to our life. [Christianity, p. 26]

I do not want to consider my existence merely as one which rises and perishes among the billions of billions of beings which constitute the universe, but as a life which has a value, if I comprehend it and live it according to true knowledge. [Christianity, p. 26]

Our generation, though so proud of its many achievements, no longer believes in the one thing which is all-essential: the spiritual advance of mankind.

[Decay, p. 65]

"Is religion a force in the spiritual life of our age?" I answer in your name and mine, "No!"

[Religion, p. 1483]

We must hold fast to the fact that religion is not a force. The proof? The war! [Religion, p. 1483]

It remains true . . . that in the war religion lost its purity, and lost its authority. It joined forces with the spirit of the world. The one victim of defeat was religion.

[Religion, p. 1483]

The religion of our age gives the same impression as an African river in the dry season—a great river bed, sand banks, and between, a small stream which seeks its way. One tries to imagine that a river once filled that bed.

[Religion, p. 1483]

If one reviews the development of religion since the middle of the nineteenth century, one understands the tragic fact that although really living religion is to be found among us, it is not the leaven that leavens the thinking of our age. [Religion, p. 1484]

That ideals, when they are brought into contact with reality, are usually crushed by facts does not mean that they are bound from the very beginning to capitulate to the facts, but merely that our ideals are not strong enough. [Childhood, p. 99f.]

The power of ideals is incalculable. We see no power in a drop of water. But let it get into a crack in the rock and be turned to ice, and it splits the rock; turned into steam, it drives the pistons of the most powerful engines. [Childhood, p. 100]

For those who through the Spirit have attained fullness of knowledge the whole panorama to its furthest ranges lies in clear daylight; for those who are "babes in Christ" only the nearest hills are visible; for those who are wise "with the wisdom of this world" all is still veiled in cloud. [Mysticism, p. 24f.]

Mysticism

Ethics must make up its mind to base itself in mysticism. [Ethics, p. 247]

Mysticism must never suppose that it exists for its own sake. It is not the blossom itself, but only the green calyx which is its support. The blossom is ethics.

[Ethics, p. 247]

Mysticism that exists for its own sake is the salt which has lost its savour. [Ethics, p. 247]

There is always the danger that the mystic will experience the eternal as absolute impassivity, and will consequently cease to regard the ethical existence as the highest manifestation of spirituality.

[Mysticism, p. 297]

The highest knowledge is to know that we are surrounded by mystery. [Christianity, p. 78]

In nature we are faced, it seems, by an insoluble enigma. The essence of the universe is full of meaning in its meaninglessness, meaningless in its fulness of meaning. [Ethics, p. 212]

All thinking must renounce the attempt to explain the universe. We cannot understand what happens in the universe. What is glorious in it is united with what is full of horror. What is full of meaning is united to what is senseless. [Religion, p. 1520]

The deeper we look into nature, the more we recognize that it is full of life, and the more profoundly we know that all life is a secret and that we are united with all life that is in nature. [Religion, p. 1520]

Every world-view not based on despair of intellectual knowledge is artificial and fictitious, for it rests on an unreliable interpretation of the world.

[Ethics, p. xiii]

Despair of any attempt to comprehend the world intellectually does not involve for me a hopeless lapse into a skepticism which would mean our drifting through life like rudderless wrecks. [Ethics, p. xiii]

We do not know what our own importance is from the point of view of the earth. How much less, then, are we able to estimate our own value or attempt to attribute to the eternal universe a meaning in which we ourselves are an end, or which is to be explained by reference to our existence. [Ethics, p. 211]

The mystery of life is always too profound for us, and . . . its value is beyond our capacity to estimate.

[Reverence, p. 233]

Only an infinitesimal part of infinite being can ever be affected by my personality. All the rest floats past me utterly indifferent to my existence, like far-away ships to which I make futile signals. [Ethics, p. 249]

The deeper piety is, the humbler are its claims with regard to knowledge of the supra-sensible. It is like a path which winds between the hills instead of going over them. [Life, p. 277]

Anyone who has recognized that the idea of Love is the spiritual beam of light which reaches us from the Infinite ceases to demand from religion that it shall offer him complete knowledge of the supra-sensible.

[Life, p. 277]

The more profound a religion is, the more it realizes this fact—that what it knows through belief is little compared with what it does not know.

[Religion, p. 1520]

We are always in the presence of mysticism when we find a human being looking upon the division between earthly and super-earthly, temporal and eternal, as transcended, and feeling himself, while still externally amid the earthly and temporal, to belong to the super-earthly and eternal. [Mysticism, p. 1]

Just as the wave has no existence of its own, but is part of the continual movement of the ocean, thus I also am destined never to experience my life as self-contained but always as part of the experience which is going on around me. [Ethics, p. 267]

When you preach the Gospel, beware of preaching it as the religion which explains everything.

[Christianity, p. 80]

Logical thought about the nature of the universe cannot reach an ethic. . . . The more it is logical and consistent, the less it has of an ethical content.

[Christianity, p. 70]

There are two kinds of *naïveté:* one which is not yet aware of all the problems and has not yet knocked at all the doors of knowledge; and another, a higher kind, which is the result of philosophy having looked into all problems, having sought counsel in all the spheres of knowledge, and then having come to see that we cannot explain anything but have to follow convictions whose inherent value appeals to us in an irresistible way.

[Christianity, p. 71f.]

Graeco-Oriental piety, Plato, the mystery-religions and the Gnostics, all alike say to man: "Free thyself from the world!" Jesus says: "Get free from the world, in order to work in this world in the spirit and in the love of God, till God transplants you into another, more perfect world." [Christianity, p. 15]

No ray of sunlight is ever lost, but the green which it wakes into existence needs time to sprout, and it is not always granted to the sower to live to see the harvest. All work that is worth anything is done in faith.

[Childhood, p. 102]

The nature of the living Being without me I can understand only through the living Being which is within me. [Life, p. 127]

It is not through knowledge, but through experience of the world that we are brought into relation with it. [Life, p. 235]

All thinking which penetrates to the depths ends in ethical mysticism. [Life, p. 235]

Ethics

Let me give you a definition of ethics: It is good to maintain life and further life; it is bad to damage and destroy life. And this ethic, profound, universal, has the significance of a religion. It *is* religion.

[Religion, p. 1521]

Ethics is the activity of man directed to secure the inner perfection of his own personality.

[Decay, p. 94]

Whoever is spared personal pain must feel himself called to help in diminishing the pain of others.

[Childhood, p. 82]

Ethics consists in this, that I experience the necessity of practising the same reverence for life toward all will-to-live, as toward my own. [Ethics, p. 254]

Ethics alone can put me in true relationship with the universe by my serving it, cooperating with it; not by trying to understand it. [Reverence, p. 234]

The maintenance of one's own life at the highest level by becoming more and more perfect in spirit, and the maintenance at the highest level of other life by sympathetic, helpful self-devotion to it—this is ethics.

[Indian, p. 260]

True ethics are world-wide. All that is ethical goes back to a single principle of morality, namely the maintenance of life at its highest level, and the furtherance of life. [Indian, p. 260]

There is a development under way by which the circle of ethics always grows wider, and ethics becomes more profound. [Religion, p. 1520f.]

Humanity has always needed ethical ideals to enable it to find the right path, that man may make the right use of the power he possesses. Today his power is increased a thousandfold. A thousandfold greater is now the need for man to possess ethical ideals to point the way.

[Religion, p. 1520]

We wander in darkness now, but one with another we all have the conviction that we are advancing to the light; that again a time will come when religion and ethical thinking will unite. [Religion, p. 1521]

In spite of the great importance we attach to the triumphs of knowledge and achievement, it is nevertheless obvious that only a humanity which is striving after ethical ends can in full measure share in the blessings brought by material progress and become master of the dangers which accompany it. [Life, p. 176f.]

To the generation which had adopted a belief in an immanent power of progress realizing itself, in some measure, naturally and automatically, and which thought that it no longer needed any ethical ideals but could advance to its goal by means of knowledge and achievement alone, terrible proof was being given by its present position of the error into which it had sunk.

[Life, p. 177]

In the Indian mind intellectualism consumes the ethical element, just as sometimes a cloud which was to have given rain is consumed in a sultry atmosphere.

[Christianity, p. 40]

In giving myself for the sake of that which comes into my tiny circle of influence, and which has need of my help, I realize the inner spiritual self-surrender to eternal being and thus lend meaning and richness to my own poor existence. The river has rejoined its ocean.

[Ethics, p. 249]

Resignation is the vestibule through which we pass in entering the palace of ethics.

[Ethics, p. 259]

Without understanding the meaning of the world I act from an inner necessity of my being so as to create values and to live ethically, in the world and exerting influence on it. [Ethics, p. xvi]

One day, in my despair, I threw myself into a chair in the consulting-room and groaned out: "What a blockhead I was to come out here to doctor savages like these!" Whereupon Joseph quietly remarked: "Yes, Doctor, here on earth you are a great blockhead, but not in heaven."

[Hospital, p. 118]

In the middle of September we get the first rains, and the cry is to bring all building timber under cover. As we have in the hospital hardly a man capable of work, I begin, assisted by two loyal helpers, to haul beams and planks about myself. Suddenly I catch sight of a negro in a white suit sitting by a patient whom he has come to visit. "Hullo! friend," I call out, "won't you lend us a hand?" "I am an intellectual and don't drag wood about," came the answer. "You're lucky," I reply. "I too wanted to become an intellectual, but I didn't succeed."

[Hospital, p. 119]

Pain is a more terrible lord of mankind than even death himself. [Edge, p. 92]

To be human means to be subject to the power of that terrible lord whose name is Pain.

[Edge, p. 171]

The Fellowship of those who bear the Mark of Pain. Who are the members of this Fellowship? Those who have learned by experience what physical pain and bodily anguish mean, belong together all the world over; they are united by a secret bond. [Edge, p. 173]

He who has been delivered from pain must not think he is now free again, and at liberty to take life up just as it was before, entirely forgetful of the past.

[Edge, p. 173]

He who has been saved by an operation from death or torturing pain, must do his part to make it possible for the kindly anaesthetic and the helpful knife to begin their work, where death and torturing pain still rule unhindered. [Edge, p. 174]

The mother who owes it to medical aid that her child still belongs to her, and not to the cold earth, must help, so that the poor mother who has never seen a doctor may be spared what she has been spared.

[Edge, p. 174]

Care for distress at home and care for distress elsewhere do but help each other if, working together, they wake men in sufficient numbers from their thoughtlessness, and call into life a new spirit of humanity.

[Edge, p. 174f.]

God does not rest content with commanding ethics. He gives it to us in our very hearts.

[Reverence, p. 239]

The voice of the true ethic is dangerous for the happy when they have the courage to listen to it.

[Ethics, p. 267f.]

To unbind what is bound, to bring the underground waters to the surface: mankind is waiting and longing for such as can do that. [Life, p. 114]

Search and see if there is not some place where you may invest your humanity. [Ethics, p. 269]

Life

Ethics is . . . reverence for the will-to-live both within and without my own personality.

[Ethics, p. 258]

There is in us an instinctive awe in the presence of life, for we ourselves are sparks of the will-to-live.

[Ethics, p. 219]

I can do no other than hold on to the fact that the will-to-live appears in me as will-to-live which aims at becoming one with other will-to-live.

[Ethics, p. 257]

In nature we encounter the eternal spirit as an enigmatic creative force. In our will-to-live we experience it in ourselves as world- and life-affirming and as ethical will. [Ethics, p. xv]

The essential nature of the will-to-live is found in this, that it is determined to live itself out. It bears in itself the impulse to realize itself to the highest possible degree of perfection. [Ethics, p. 222]

In delicate blossoms, in the manifold wondrous forms of the jelly-fish, in a blade of grass, in the crystal; everywhere the will-to-live strives to reach that perfection which is implicit in its own nature.

[Ethics, p. 222]

Whenever my life has given itself out in any way for other life, my eternal will-to-live experiences union with the eternal, since all life is one. I possess a cordial which secures me from dying of thirst in the desert of life.

[Ethics, p. 257]

The will-to-live which aspires to knowledge of the objective world is sure to make shipwreck, the will-to-live which aspires to knowledge of itself is a bold and skilful sailor. [Ethics, p. 221]

The will-to-live is not a flame which burns only when it has the fuel of events which it desires; it even gives a purer clearer light when it has to depend on itself for nourishment. [Ethics, p. 223]

The Indian idea of the divine is, that it is pure, spiritual essence. It is the ocean into which man, tired of swimming, wishes to sink. The God of the Gospel of Jesus is living, ethical Will, desiring to give to my will a new direction. He says to me: "Strike out courageously! Do not ask where your efforts will take you on the infinite ocean. It is my will that you should swim."

[Christianity, p. 38]

The way to true mysticism leads us through and beyond rational reflection to profound experience of the world and of our will-to-live. [Ethics, p. xviii]

Every conviction which possesses real value is non-rational and enthusiastic in character, since it cannot be the product of knowledge about the universe, but arises from the reflective experience of the will-to-live, in virtue of which we leave behind all mere intellectual knowledge of the world. [Ethics, p. xviii]

My knowledge of the world is a knowledge from the outside and must always remain incomplete. The knowledge derived from my will-to-live is, on the contrary, direct, and goes back to the secret springs of life as life exists in itself. [Ethics, p. 221]

True resignation is not a becoming weary of the world, rather it is the quiet triumph over the circumstances of life which the will-to-live enjoys in its bitterest need. [Ethics, p. 224]

Every diminution of the will-to-live is an act of insincerity towards oneself or a definite symptom of ill-health. [Ethics, p. 221]

I do not say, "I am life"; for life continues to be a mystery too great to understand. I only know that I cling to it. I fear its cessation—death. I dread its diminution—pain. I seek its enlargement—joy.

[Reverence, p. 228]

Reverence

Ethics is nothing else than reverence for life. [Ethics, p. xvi]

Reverence for life is a universal ethic. [Reverence, p. 233]

Reverence for life affords me my fundamental principle of morality, namely that good consists in maintaining, assisting and enhancing life, and that to destroy, to harm or to hinder life is evil. [Ethics, p. xvi]

It is *good* to maintain and cherish life; it is *evil* to destroy and to check life. [Ethics, p. 254]

Evil is what annihilates, hampers, or hinders life. [Reverence, p. 230]

It is in reverence for life that knowledge passes over into experience. [Ethics, p. xv]

What we call love is in its essence reverence for life. [Indian, p. 260]

My life bears its meaning in itself. And this meaning is to be found in living out the highest and most worthy idea which my will-to-live can furnish . . . the idea of reverence for life. [Ethics, p. xvi]

To have reverence in the face of life is to be in the grip of the eternal, unoriginated, forward-pushing will, which is the foundation of all being.

[Ethics, p. 223]

Reverence for life drives a man on as the whirling, thrashing screw forces a ship through the water.

[Ethics, p. 256]

Reverence for life raises us above all intellectual knowledge of external objects, and grafts us on to the tree which is assured against drought because it is planted by the rivers of water. [Ethics, p. 223]

All vital religious feeling flows from reverence for life and for the necessity and for the need for ideals which is implicit in life. [Ethics, p. 223]

The ethic of reverence for life is the ethic of Jesus brought to philosophical expression, extended into cosmical form, and conceived as intellectually necessary.

[Ethics, p. 258]

The ethical mysticism of Reverence for Life is rationalism thought to a conclusion. [Life, p. 235]

The question which haunts men and women today is whether life is worth living. [Reverence, p. 228]

Humanitarianism consists in this principle, that a *man* is never to be sacrificed for an *end*.

[Ethics, p. 234]

Reverence for life does not allow me to appropriate my own happiness. [Ethics, p. 267]

Reverence for life does not allow the scholar to live for his science alone, even if he is very useful to the community in so doing. It does not permit the artist to exist only for his art, even if he gives inspiration to many by its means. It refuses to let the business man imagine that he fulfils all legitimate demands in the course of his business activities. It demands from all that they should sacrifice a portion of their own lives for others.

[Ethics, p. 269]

The ethic of reverence for life constrains all, in whatever walk of life they may find themselves, to busy themselves intimately with all the human and vital processes which are being played out around them, and to give themselves as men to the man who needs human help and sympathy. [Ethics, p. 269]

Everything which in the usual ethical valuation of interhuman relations is looked upon as good can be traced back to the material and spiritual maintenance or enhancement of human life and to the effort to raise it to its highest level of value. [Ethics, p. 254]

Everything in human relations which is considered as evil, is in the final analysis found to be material or spiritual destruction or checking of human life and slackening of the effort to raise it to its highest value.

[Ethics, p. 254]

Regarding the question of property, the ethic of reverence for life is outspokenly individualist in the sense that goods earned or inherited are to be placed at the disposition of the community, not according to any standards whatever laid down by society, but according to the absolutely free decision of the individual.

[Ethics, p. 266]

Those who have very little that they can call their own are in most danger of becoming purely egoistic. A deep truth lies in the parable of Jesus, which makes the servant who had received least the least faithful of all. [Ethics, p. 266]

Reverence for life places all its hopes on the enhancement of the feeling of responsibility in men. It defines possessions as the property of the community, of which the individual is sovereign steward.

[Ethics, p. 266]

The world-view of Reverence for Life follows from taking the world as it is. And the world means the horrible in the glorious, the meaningless in the full of meaning, the sorrowful in the joyful. However it is looked at it remains to many a riddle. [Life, p. 235]

Sometime or another all of us must have found that happy events have not been able to make us happy, nor unhappy events to make us unhappy. There is within each of us a modulation, an inner exaltation, which lifts us above the buffetings with which events assail us.

[Reverence, p. 229]

Reverence for Life brings us into a spiritual relation with the world which is independent of all knowledge of the universe. Through the dark valley of resignation it leads us by an inward necessity up to the shining heights of ethical world- and life-affirmation. [Life, p. 235]

The stronger the reverence for natural life, the stronger grows also that for spiritual life.

[Life, p. 270]

To the man who is truly ethical all life is sacred, including that which from the human point of view seems lower on the scale. [Life, p. 271]

Ethics are in their unqualified form extended responsibility with regard to everything that has life.

[Ethics, p. 255]

Ethics are boundless in their domain and limitless in their demands. They are concerned with all living things that come within our sphere.

[Indian, p. 260]

A man is ethical only when life, as such, is sacred to him, that of plants and animals as that of his fellowmen, and when he devotes himself helpfully to all life that is in need of help. [Life, p. 188]

Only by serving every kind of life do I enter the service of that Creative Will whence all life emanates.

[Reverence, p. 234]

A man is really ethical only when he obeys the constraint laid on him to help all life which he is able to succor, and when he goes out of his way to avoid injuring anything living. [Ethics, p. 254]

Wherever any animal is forced into the service of man, the sufferings which it has to bear on that account are the concern of every one of us.

[Ethics, p. 264]

The countryman who has mowed down a thousand blossoms in his meadow as fodder for his cows should take care that on the way home he does not, in wanton pastime, switch off the head of a single flower growing on the edge of the road, for in so doing he injures life without being forced to do so by necessity.

[Ethics, p. 264]

It is the fate of every truth to be an object of ridicule when it is first acclaimed. [Ethics, p. 255]

The traveler on the plain sees from afar the distant range of mountains. Then he loses sight of them again. His way winds slowly upwards through the valleys, drawing ever nearer to the peaks, until at last, at a turn of the path, they stand before him, not in the shapes which they had seemed to take from the distant plain, but in their actual forms. [Quest, p. 23]

BIOGRAPHICAL DATA

(Compiled from reminiscences shared with the editor during long and pleasant evenings in Dr. Schweitzer's study-office-bedroom at Lambarene, Gabon, French Equatorial Africa.)

January 14, 1875. Born at Kaysersberg, Haute Alsace. During this year his father became pastor at Gunsbach, in the Munster Valley, Haute Alsace.

1880–1884. In the village school.

Autumn 1884 to autumn 1885. Realschule at Munster.

Autumn 1885 to August 1893. Gymnasium at Mulhouse, Haute Alsace.

June 18, 1893. Passed his matriculation examination for the university at the Mulhouse Gymnasium.

October, 1893. First sojourn in Paris. Studied the organ under Widor.

November 1893 to spring 1898. Student at the University of Strassburg in theology, philosophy, and musical theory, living in the Theological Seminary of St. Thomas (Collegium Wilhelmitanum). While at the university wrote his first book, a small brochure in French upon the life and activity of Eugène Munch, his former organ teacher at Mulhouse, who died of typhoid fever at the beginning of his career, a book intended for the friends and pupils of this artist. The book was printed at Mulhouse in 1898.

April 1, 1894 to April 1, 1895. Military service in infantry regiment 143.

Autumn 1897. Wrote thesis required of all candidates for the first examination in theology upon the topic prescribed by the faculty: "The Idea of the Last Supper in Daniel Schleiermacher, Compared with the Ideas of Luther, Zwingli and Calvin." In studying Schleiermacher's idea of the Last Supper he was struck by the fact that Schleiermacher insisted that Jesus did not ask the disciples to repeat this meal, and that the disciples had done so of their own initiative.

May 6, 1898. Passed his first theological examination before the faculty. The examination consisted of four written papers on the New Testament, the Old Testament, Church History and Dogmatics; an oral examination in five parts, New

Testament, Old Testament, Church History, Dogmatics and Practical Theology; and a sermon preached in a church with two of the examiners present. As a result of this examination he received the Goll Scholarship, the recipient of which was pledged to take his licentiate in theology at Strassburg within six years or return the money received.

Summer 1898. Continued to study philosophy at the University of Strassburg under Ziegler and Windelband. At the end of the summer he proposed to Professor Ziegler as the theme of his doctoral thesis a study of Kant's philosophy of religion in relation to the different stages of what seemed to him its constant evolution. At this time he was not living at the Theological Seminary.

Autumn 1898 to spring 1899. Student at the Sorbonne in Paris, living at 20 Rue de la Sorbonne. He neglected the courses at the college, devoting himself to his organ studies under Widor, and to his thesis on Kant. He paid almost no attention to the books about Kant, confining his attention to a minute study of the text and the language peculiarities, in order to discover the different stages in the development of the thought of Kant which was in a state of constant flux.

March 12, 1899. Returned to Gunsbach and revised his manuscript.

April to July, 1899. At Berlin for the study of philosophy and organ.

End of July, 1899. Returned to Strassburg for his examination in philosophy with Windelband and Ziegler.

Autumn of 1899. Returned to his old room in the Collegium Wilhelmitanum (St. Thomas Foundation) as a paying guest.

December 1, 1899. Appointed Lehr-Vicar at St. Nicholas in Strassburg, in compliance with the rules requiring a student to serve in a church for a period between his first and second theological examination. There were two aged pastors at the church, Gerold who was the leader of the liberal party, and Knittel in whom orthodoxy and pietism mingled. Schweitzer began to work on a thesis upon the historical origin of the Last Supper, to submit in fulfillment of the requirements for the degree of licentiate in Theology which one had to have to become a Privat-Dozent. This study led him to new conceptions about Jesus' messianic consciousness and his idea of sacrifice. At the same time Schweitzer worked on another book, *Das Messianitäts- und Leidensgeheimnis Jesu.* (The Secret of the Messiahship and Passion of Jesus.)

End of December, 1899. *Die Religionsphilosophie Kants von der Kritik der reinen Vernunft bis zur Religion innerhalb der Grenzen der blossen Vernunft* (*The Religious Philosophy of Kant from the "Critique of Pure Reason" to "Religion within the Bounds of Mere Reason"*), published by J. C. B. Mohr, at Tübingen, to whom Professor Holtsmann had recommended the book. Schweitzer received from the editor about 600 marks and the copies which he had to furnish to the faculty.

July 15, 1900. Passed second theological examination before a commission of learned pastors among whom sat a member of the faculty. The subjects were the same as in the first examination except that more emphasis was placed on practical theology. Busy with his studies of the Last Supper and the messianic consciousness of Jesus, he had not taken the time to review his previous studies in the various fields of theology and barely passed the examination.

July 21, 1900. Obtained the degree of licentiate in Theology with his study of the Last Supper. To obtain this degree he also had to pass a very difficult colloquium before a commission of the faculty. Schweitzer passed "magna cum laude."

September 23, 1900. Ordained at St. Nicholas as a regular curate.

May 1, 1901 to September 30, 1901. Received provisional appointment as Principal of the Theological Seminary (Collegium Wilhelmitanum) upon the death of Erichson until Gustav Anrich could assume the office.

1901. *Das Abendmahlproblem auf Grund der wissenschaftlichen Forschung des 19. Jahrhunderts und der historischen Berichte* (*The Problem of the Last Supper in the Light of Nineteenth Century Scientific Research and of the Historical Documents*), published by J. C. B. Mohr at Tübingen. The American edition was published by Dodd, Mead and Company in New York, under the title *The Mystery of the Kingdom of God*, and the English edition by A. and C. Black in 1925 in London.

1902. Appointed Privat-Dozent, thanks to the influence of Professor Holtzmann, and gave his inaugural lectures before the faculty upon the structure and tendencies of the Fourth Gospel. There followed in the summer of this year his first regular course on the Pastoral Epistles.

October 1, 1903. Received permanent appointment as Principal of the Theological Seminary, when Anrich was appointed Extraordinarius in Church History in succession to Ernst Lucius, who had suddenly died. Moved from the city to his official quarters on the Embankment of St. Thomas, using earlier student room for his study. Received stipend of 2400 marks.

January 14, 1905. Thirtieth birthday. Decided to devote the rest of his life to the natives of equatorial Africa as a doctor of medicine.

1905. *J. S. Bach, le musicien-poète* (J. S. Bach, the Musician-Poet) published by Costallat in Paris, and in 1908 by Breitkopf & Härtel in Leipzig. The German edition was not a translation of the French book, but an entirely new work. The first chapter had been written in Bayreuth in 1905. Published also in English under the title *J. S. Bach.*

October 13, 1905. Made known his decision to serve as a missionary doctor, and entered into discussion with the Paris Missionary Society.

Spring 1906. Resigned from the directorship of the Theological Seminary. Went to live in the mansard story of the house occupied by Dr. Curtius, the president of the Superior Consistory, in the same block of buildings with the Theological Seminary. There were three small rooms and a kitchen.

1906 to 1913. Studied as a medical student at the University of Strassburg.

1906. Published *Von Reimarus zu Wrede. Eine Geschichte der Leben-Jesu-Forschung* (*From Reimarus to Wrede. A History of Research in the Life of Jesus*), (J. C. B. Mohr, Tübingen). Reimarus had been the first to emphasize the eschatological in Jesus, and Wrede, who died in 1907, had tried to eliminate all eschatology and all messianic ideas from the thought world of Jesus. The English edition, under the title *The Quest of the Historical Jesus*, was published in London by A. & C. Black in 1910. This year there also appeared the treatise, *Deutsche und französische Orgelbaukunst und Orgelkunst* (German and French Organ-Building and Organ-Playing), published by Breitkopf & Härtel, in Leipzig.

1906 to 1912. In the very restricted leisure moments left by his medical studies, his services as curate at St. Nicholas, his concert tours, and a very heavy correspondence he began his study of the Pauline ideas. He was trying to find out how Paul, beginning with primitive, eschatological Christianity, arrived at a mysticism of dying and being born again "in Jesus Christ," and how this eschatological mysticism prepared the way for the hellenization of Christianity in the mysticism of "being in the Logos." He hoped to be able to finish the book before his departure for Africa, but succeeded only in completing the introduction, a history of the various interpretations of the writings of St. Paul. The completion of his work was delayed by three other tasks. Towards the end of this period of medical study he prepared in collaboration with Widor an edition of Bach's organ works. He was, secondly, engaged in enlarging and completing the second edition of his *Geschichte der Leben-Jesu-Forschung.* To do this he had to go through a great many new books, and particularly to study the whole question of the historical existence of Jesus, which had been brought to the fore by Drews. Thirdly, he was engaged in preparing his thesis for the degree of doctor of medicine, a study of the books which dealt with the question of Jesus' mentality from a psychiatric point of view. This book necessitated a profound study of psychiatric questions, and completed his history of the written lives of Jesus.

1911. His *Geschichte der Paulinischen Forschung von der Reformation bis auf die Gegenwart* (*History of the Study of Paul from the Reformation to the Present Time*) was published by J. C. B. Mohr at Tübingen. The English edition under the title of *Paul and His Interpreters* was published by A. & C. Black in London in 1912. This book bore the dedication "Der medizinischen Fakultät der Universität Strassburg in tiefer Dankbarkeit für die gewährte Gastfreundschaft."

Autumn 1911. Played the organ for Widor's Second Symphony for Organ and Orchestra at the Festival of French Music at Munich.

Autumn to December 1911. Passed his examination in medicine at Strassburg, during a period of terrible exhaustion.

Spring 1912. Resigned his posts as a teacher in the university and as a preacher at St. Nicholas. His last lectures were on the evaluation of religion from the point of view of historical criticism and the natural sciences.

June 18, 1912. Married Helene Bresslau, daughter of the Strassburg historian. Afterwards retired to his father's house in Gunsbach to work on the second edition of his *Geschichte der Leben-Jesu-Forschung*, assisted by his wife.

February 1913. Having completed his year of internship, and having finished his thesis, he received the degree of doctor of medicine.

March 26, 1913. Embarked at Bordeaux for Africa, where he established a hospital on the grounds of the Lambarene station of the Paris Missionary Society. The place was called Andende.

1913. The second edition of his *Geschichte der Leben-Jesu-Forschung* was published by J. C. B. Mohr at Tübingen. In the same year J. C. B. Mohr published in Tübingen *Die Psychiatrische Beurteilung Jesu* (The Psychiatric Study of Jesus). The proofs of the former book were corrected on the train from Paris to Bordeaux, where he was to embark for Africa. The proofs of the latter were corrected by a friend in Strassburg while Schweitzer was at sea. Six volumes in the edition of Bach's works were finished before his departure. The last three volumes of choral compositions were completed in Africa during the first few months after his arrival there, but for various reasons these volumes have not yet been published.

August 5 to end of November 1914. Interned with his wife at Lambarene as an enemy alien. Began his work on *The Philosophy of Civilization*, about which he had been thinking since the summer of 1899, and which an editor in England had requested about 1910. This work was continued even after November when he was allowed more liberty to continue his hospital work.

September 1915. During a two-hundred-kilometer journey up the Ogowe River to N'Gomo, suddenly the words "Reverence for Life" came to him as the elementary and universal conception of ethics for which he had been seeking. Upon this principle his whole philosophy of civilization was subsequently based.

September 1917. Transferred with his wife to France as a civil intern. At Garaison in the Pyrénées continued to work on his philosophy.

Spring 1918. Transferred to St. Rémy de Provence. Served as a doctor during the daytime and worked on his philosophy during the evenings.

End of July 1918. Returned to Alsace in an exchange of prisoners.

1919 to 1921. Accepted a post as preacher at St. Nicholas, and also a post as physician in the City Hospital of Strassburg. Occupied the empty parsonage on the Nicholas Embankment through the courtesy of the Chapter of St. Thomas. Submitted to operation, from which he did not fully recover for two years.

January 14, 1919. Daughter born on his birthday.

About Christmas 1919. Received invitation to give course of lectures at Uppsala in Sweden.

After Easter 1920. Delivered lectures on the Olaus-Petri Foundation at the University of Uppsala, using as his subject the problem of world- and life-affirmation and ethics in philosophy and world-religions, working up the material afresh, as he had left his manuscripts in Africa. Gave a series of organ concerts and lectures in Sweden to pay off the debts which he had incurred for the hospital.

Middle July 1920. Returned to Strassburg to write in a few weeks a book on his experiences in Africa, which the editor Lindblad at Uppsala had requested.

1920. Honorary doctorate from theological faculty in Zürich. The Swedish edition of *Zwischen Wasser und Urwald* (*Between the Water and the Jungle*) was published by Lindblad at Uppsala. This book was published in German in 1921 by Paul Haupt at Berne, and in 1925 also by C. H. Beck in Munich. Published in English under the title *On the Edge of the Primeval Forest.*

Spring 1921. Played the organ at the Orféo Català in Barcelona for the first production of the St. Matthew Passion in Spain.

April 1921. Gave up both positions at Strassburg depending thenceforth for his support on his pen and his organ. Returned to Gunsbach, where he was appointed vicar to his father, in order to work quietly on his *Philosophy of Civilization.* Retained a room in Strassburg on the rue de l'Ail (Knoblauchgasse).

Autumn 1921. In Switzerland.

November 1921. In Sweden.

January and February 1922. Courses of lectures in England at Oxford at Mansfield College on Dale Foundation, and at the Selly-Oak Colleges at Birmingham on "Christianity and the World-Religions," and at Cambridge on "The Meaning of Eschatology," and at the Society for the Science of Religion in London on "The Pauline Problem." Also gave a series of organ concerts in England.

Spring 1922. Three more weeks of lectures and concerts in Sweden, followed by lectures and concerts in Switzerland.

Summer 1922. Working undisturbed on *The Philosophy of Civilization.*

Autumn 1922. More lectures and concerts in Switzerland, a series of lectures in Copenhagen on the invitation of the theological faculty, followed by lectures and concerts in various Danish cities.

January 1923. Spoke in Prague on *The Philosophy of Civilization.*

Spring 1923. *The Philosophy of Civilization* published by C. H. Beck in Munich and Paul Haupt in Berne in 1923 in two volumes, I. *The Decay and Restoration of Civilization*, and II. *Civilization and Ethics*. Also in the same year Allen and Unwin published in London *Christianity and the World-Religions*. The German edition appeared in 1924 with Paul Haupt in Berne.

February 1924. Wrote *Memoirs of Childhood and Youth.* The English edition was published by Allen and Unwin in London the same year.

February 14, 1924. Left Strassburg for Africa, leaving his wife behind in Europe because of her poor health. Carried with him preliminary drafts of his book on *The Mysticism of Paul the Apostle* on which he had been working during all the years of his first sojourn in Africa and during his sojourn in Europe from 1917 to 1924.

April 19, 1924 to July 21, 1927. Second sojourn in Africa. Compelled to reconstruct the hospital, which had fallen into ruin, and later to transfer it to a new and roomier site at Adolinanongo, where the new buildings were constructed of hardwood and corrugated iron. During this period of rebuilding he was compelled to abandon all literary work. In the morning he worked as a doctor, in the afternoon as a laborer. The number of patients constantly increased and he was obliged to send to Europe for two more doctors and two more nurses. Just as he was about to resume work on *The Mysticism of Paul the Apostle* a severe famine and an epidemic of dysentery set in, and again his writing had to be abandoned. He was able, however, to keep up his regular practice on his piano with organ pedals. Reports of his work in Africa were sent to Europe in the form of letters to friends and supporters and published in three small volumes, under the title *Mitteilungen aus Lambarene* (Reports from Lambarene), by C. H. Beck in Munich and Paul Haupt in Berne. The first covered the period from spring to autumn 1924, and appeared in 1925; the second the period from autumn 1924 to autumn 1925, and appeared in 1926; and the third the period from autumn 1925 to summer 1927, and appeared in 1928.

July 1927 to December 1929. In Europe. Lectures and concert tours in Sweden, Denmark, Holland, Germany, Switzerland, England, and Czechoslovakia. During this period devoted all his spare time to his book on *The Mysticism of Paul the Apostle.* A large part of this book was written in Königsfeld in the Black Forest, where he had established a summer home. The book was finished on the boat which took him back to Africa.

August 28, 1928. Received Goethe Prize from the City of Frankfort, delivering an address there on his indebtedness to Goethe. This was the second time that this prize had been awarded, Stephan George having been the first to receive it. With the money he received he built a home in Gunsbach where he planned also to house the personnel of his hospital while on vacation in Europe. Schweitzer's address on Goethe was published by Henry Holt in New York in 1929, following the text published in the *Hibbert Journal* in July of the same year.

December 26, 1929 to January 7, 1932. Third sojourn in Africa. During this sojourn he wrote his autobiography. In 1929 he had written for the editor Felix Meiner in Leipzig a brief autobiographical sketch for the seventh volume of his *Philosophie der Gegenwart in Selbstdarstellungen* (Present Day Philosophy in Self-Portraits). This particular chapter was republished by the editor as a small book, but as Schweitzer considered that readers might consider this a real autobiography and draw false conclusions from it, he decided to enlarge it to include a review of his life and his literary works. The book appeared in German under the title *Aus meinem Leben und Denken,* published by Felix Meiner in Leipzig in 1931, and the following year it was published in England under the title *Out of My Life and Thought.* Upon the completion of the autobiography, Schweitzer continued his work on the third volume of his *Philosophy of Civilization.* This work in turn was interrupted by an invitation received in October 1931, from the bürgermeister of Frankfort to deliver a memorial address on the anniversary of the death of Goethe. The acceptance of this invitation necessitated an earlier return to Europe than he had contemplated. The first draft of the address was prepared at Lambarene towards the close of 1931 and the address was completed on the steamer that took him to Europe in January 1932.

1931. *More from the Primeval Forest* was published in England by A. & C. Black. This was a translation of the German book *Das Urwaldspital zu Lambarene*, which had been published by Beck at Munich in 1931. This latter book in turn brought together into a single volume the three little books, *Mitteilungen aus Lambarene*, which had been published in 1925, 1926, and 1928. The American edition, published by Henry Holt and Company in New York, bore the title, *The Forest Hospital at Lambarene*.

February 1932 to April 1933. In Europe. Lectures and concerts in Holland, England, Sweden, Germany and Switzerland. Worked on the third volume of *The Philosophy of Civilization*, completing the plan for the whole book and sketching out the different chapters.

March 22, 1932. Memorial address in Frankfort on 100th anniversary of death of Goethe. The address was published in the same year by C. H. Beck in Munich.

April 21, 1933 to January 11, 1934. Fourth sojourn in Africa. All of his leisure was employed upon the third volume of his philosophy, and in preparation of the Gifford Lectures which were to be given in 1934 and 1935.

February 1934 to February 1935. In Europe. The spring and summer were spent upon the third volume and upon the preparation of the Gifford Lectures.

Autumn 1934. Hibbert Lectures at Manchester College, Oxford, under the subject "Religion in Modern Civilization." These lectures were later repeated at London University College. They have not yet been published, but a fairly adequate summary of them was printed in *The Christian Century* in November 1934.

November 1934. Gifford Lectures at Edinburgh, in which he endeavored to trace the progress of human thought from the great thinkers of India, China, Greece, and Persia. The chapter upon the evolution of Indian thought grew to such an extent that he decided to publish it as a separate book. It was issued under the German title of *Die Weltanschauung der indischen Denker* (*The World View of the Indian Thinkers*) by Beck at Munich in 1934; under the French title *Les Grands*

Penseurs de l'Inde (*The Great Indian Thinkers*) by Payot at Paris in 1936; and under the English title *Indian Thought and Its Development* by Hodder and Stoughton at London in 1936. The same year it was published by Henry Holt and Company in New York.

February 26, 1935 to August 22, 1935. Fifth sojourn in Africa. This stay was terminated by his obligation to return to Europe for the second series of Gifford Lectures, which were largely written in Africa.

September 1935 to February 1937. In Europe.

November 1935. Second course of Gifford Lectures. Lectures and concerts in England.

1936. Working on his philosophy, translating into French his book *Les Grands Penseurs de l'Inde*, and in October making records of organ music for Columbia Records in London upon the organ of St. Aurelia's at Strassburg.

February 18, 1937 to January 10, 1939. Sixth sojourn in Africa. He carried with him the manuscript for his philosophy, believing that now at last he would be able to finish it, but the increasing responsibilities of the hospital left him little leisure. For some time he thought that the volume of material would make it necessary to publish two volumes instead of one. He could not bring himself to this decision, however, and finally set to work to compress his thought into the compass of a single book. In order to simplify the problem he then planned to publish separately the chapters on the Chinese thinkers in whom he had become deeply interested.

1938. Wrote *From My African Notebook*, a little volume of anecdotes upon the ideas and the lives of the natives. Meiner of Leipzig published it under the title of *Afrikanische Geschichten* (*African Stories*) in 1938; Payot in Paris issued the French edition in 1941; Allen and Unwin in London issued the English edition in 1938.

January 10, 1939. Left for Europe with the hope of completing his third volume.

February 1939. Arrived in Europe, only to decide that war could not be avoided, and might break out at any moment. Decided, therefore, to return immediately to Africa.

February 12, 1939. Embarked again for Africa.

March 3, 1939 to October 1948. Seventh sojourn in Africa. During the first two years of the war he was able to work continuously on his book, but afterwards the lack of white personnel at the hospital made it necessary for him to devote himself almost exclusively to the care of the sick and to other hospital duties. Toward the end of 1945 he wrote an account of the war years at Lambarene, which was published in 1946 in Switzerland, Alsace, England and America, under the title *Lambarene 1939–1945*. The close of the war brought little relief, and it was not until 1947 that a rather more adequate personnel became available. Dr. Schweitzer then began to plan for his long-delayed return to Europe, but his departure from Africa did not take place until the fall of 1948. Just before his departure he wrote a little summary of the history of the hospital, which was published in Switzerland with photographs by Dr. Wildikann, one of the women who had spent some years with him in Africa, under the title *Das Spital im Urwald* (The Hospital in the Primeval Forest).

October 1948 to October 1949. In Europe with his wife at Königsberg in the Black Forest, and at his home in Gunsbach, Alsace. During this sojourn in Europe he saw his four grandchildren for the first time in Switzerland. Working on a theological book and on the third volume of his *Philosophy of Civilization*. Made his first visit to America to give the principal address on Goethe for the Goethe Foundation at Aspen, Colorado, in July 1949, visiting New York, Chicago and Boston. Returned to Africa in October 1949.

BIBLIOGRAPHY

OF THE WRITINGS OF ALBERT SCHWEITZER

I. AUTOBIOGRAPHICAL

African Notebook. Translated by Mrs. C. E. B. Russell. New York: Henry Holt and Company, 1939.

Afrikanische Jagdgeschichten. Strasbourg: Editions des Sources, 1936.

Memoirs of Childhood and Youth. Translated by C. T. Campion. New York: The Macmillan Company, 1931.

Mitteilungen aus Lambarene. Three booklets.
1—1924. Bern: Paul Haupt, 1925.
2—1924–25. Bern: Paul Haupt, 1926.
3—1925–27. Bern: Paul Haupt, 1928.

On the Edge of the Primeval Forest and *The Forest Hospital at Lambarene.* Both translated by C. T. Campion. Combined in one volume. New York: The Macmillan Company, 1948.

Out of My Life and Thought. Translated by C. T. Campion. New York: Henry Holt and Company, 1948.

Selbstdarstellung. In Volume VII of *Die Philosophie der Gegenwart in Selbstdarstellungen*, edited by Dr. Raymund Schmidt. Leipzig: Felix Meiner, 1929.

Das Spital im Urwald. Bern: Paul Haupt, 1948.

II. BIOGRAPHICAL

Eugène Munch. Mulhouse, Alsace: Brinkmann, 1898.

Goethe: Four Studies. Translated by Charles R. Joy. Boston: The Beacon Press, 1949.

III. RELIGION AND THEOLOGY

Christianity and the Religions of the World. Translated by Joanna Powers. New York: Henry Holt and Company, 1939.

The Mystery of the Kingdom of God. Translated by Walter Lowrie. New York: Dodd, Mead & Company, 1914.

The Mysticism of Paul the Apostle. Translated by W. Montgomery. New York: Henry Holt and Company, 1931.

Paul and His Interpreters. Translated by W. Montgomery. New York: The Macmillan Company, 1912.

The Quest of the Historical Jesus: A Critical Study of Its Progress from Reimarus to Wrede. Translated by W. Montgomery. New York: The Macmillan Company, 1945.

IV. PHILOSOPHY AND ETHICS

Civilization and Ethics. Being Part II of *The Philosophy of Civilization.* Translated by C. T. Campion. New York: The Macmillan Company, 1929.

The Decay and Restoration of Civilization. Being Part I of *The Philosophy of Civilization.* Translated by C. T. Campion. New York: The Macmillan Company, 1932.

Indian Thought and Its Development. Translated by Mrs. C. E. B. Russell. New York: Henry Holt and Company, 1936.

Die Religionsphilosophie Kants von der Kritik der reinen Vernunft bis zur Religion innerhalb der Grenzen der blossen Vernunft. Tübingen: J. C. B. Mohr (Paul Siebeck), 1899.

V. PSYCHIATRY

The Psychiatric Study of Jesus. Translated by Charles R. Joy. Boston: The Beacon Press, 1948.

VI. MUSIC

Deutsche und französische Orgelbaukunst und Orgelkunst. Leipzig: Breitkopf und Härtel, 1927.

Johann Sebastian Bach. Translated by Ernest Newman. 2 volumes. New York: The Macmillan Company, 1947.

VII. ARTICLES AND PAMPHLETS

"Busy Days in Lambaréné." *The Christian Century,* Vol. LI (March 14, 1934), pp. 355–57.

"Einführung in das Schaffen Bachs." Introduction to Selection of the Best Piano Works of Johann Sebastian Bach. In *Klassiker der Tonkunst.* Vienna and Leipzig: Universal-Edition A. G.

"The Ethics of Reverence for Life." *Christendom,* Vol. I, No. 2 (Winter, 1936), pp. 225–39.

"Gutachten über die Orgel zu St. Jacobi in Hamburg." In *Die Schnitger-Orgel der Hauptkirche St. Jacobi in Hamburg,* by Karl Mehrkens, pp. 15 f. Kassel: Im Bärenreiter-Verlag, 1930.

"Im Lande der Schlangen." *Evangelischer Familien Kalender für Elsass-Lothringen*, 1939.

"Josephine das zahme Wildschwein." *Schweizerisches Jahrbuch, Die Ernte*. Published by the Garbe-Schriftleitung. Basel: Friedrich Reinhardt, 1923.

"Letter from Lambaréné." *The Living Age*, Vol. CCCLV (September, 1938), pp. 70 ff.

"Mes Souvenirs sur Cosima Wagner." *L'Alsace Française*, Vol. XXV, No. 7 (February 12, 1933), pp. 124 f.

"M. J. Erb's Symphonie für Orchester und Orgel" and "Ch. M. Widor's Sinfonia Sacra für Orgel und Orchester." Both in *Die Strassburger Sängerhaus-Orgel*. Strassburg: Julius Manias und Cie.

"Nochmals Falkenjägerei." *Atlantis*, March, 1932. Zürich: Atlantis Verlag.

"The One-Talent People." *The Christian Herald*, Vol. LXII (September, 1949), p. 24.

"Ein Pelikan erzählt aus seinem Laben." *Atlantis*, February, 1948. Zürich: Atlantis Verlag.

"Die Philosophie und die allgemeine Bildung im neunzehnten Jahrhundert." One of 24 essays on the nineteenth century in *Das neunzehnte Jahrhundert*, pp. 61–68. Strassburg, 1900.

"Philosophy and the Movement for the Protection of Animals." Edinburgh: *International Journal of Animal Protection*, May, 1935.

"Regen und schönes Wetter auf dem Äquator." *Kirchenkalender*.

"The Relations of the White and Colored Races." *The Contemporary Review*, Vol. CXXXIII, No. 745 (January, 1928), pp. 65–70.

"Religion and Modern Civilization." *The Christian Century*, Vol. LI, No. 47 (November 21, 1934), pp. 1483–84; No. 48 (November 28, 1934), pp. 1519–21.

"Der runde Violinbogen." *Schweizerische Musikzeitung*, No. 6, 1933.

"Le Secours Médical aux Colonies." *Revue des Deux Mondes*, Series 8, Vol. V (September 15, 1931), pp. 390–404.

"Sermon on Forgiveness." *The Christian World*, November 1, 1934, p. 11.

"Siegfried Ochs als Bachinterpret." *Fest-Program des Berliner Philharmonischen Chors*, December 5, 1932, pp. 11–13.

"Souvenirs d'Ernest Münch." *Le Choeur de St. Guillaume de*

Strasbourg: Un Chapitre de l'Histoire de la Musique en Alsace, compiled by Erik Jung, pp. 51–62. Strasbourg: P.H. Heitz, 1947.

"Souvenirs et Appréciations." *Un Grand Musicien Français: Marie-Joseph Erb,* pp. 83–88. Strasbourg-Paris: Editions F.-X. Le Roux & Cie., 1948.

"Sunday at Lambaréné." *The Christian Century,* Vol. XLVIII (March 18, 1931), pp. 540–41.

"En Välgörare för de Primitiva Invånarna i Ogowes Urskogar." Uppsala: J. A. Lindblads Förlag, 1933.

"Warum es so schwer ist in Paris einen guten Chor zusammenzubringen." *Die Musik,* Vol. IX, No. 19. Berlin: Bernhard Schuster.

"Zur Reform des Orgelbaues." *Monatschrift für Gottesdienst und kirchliche Kunst,* Vol. XXXII, No. 6 (June, 1927), pp. 148–54.

VIII. Anthologies

Albert Schweitzer: An Anthology. Edited with an introduction and a chronological summary of Dr. Schweitzer's life by Charles R. Joy. New York: Harper and Brothers; Boston: The Beacon Press, 1947.

The Wit and Wisdom of Albert Schweitzer. A book of epigrams compiled with an introduction by Charles R. Joy. Boston: The Beacon Press, 1949.

Note: Dr. Schweitzer's books have been published in a number of different languages, in addition to the original French or German in which they were written. The same book has occasionally been published in England and America under different English titles. Sometimes the English translation is an abridgment of the original text. No effort has been made to make the above bibliography complete for all languages and all editions. It lists books and articles in languages other than English only when no English translation has been made, and lists in English only the one American edition which seems to the editor most convenient.

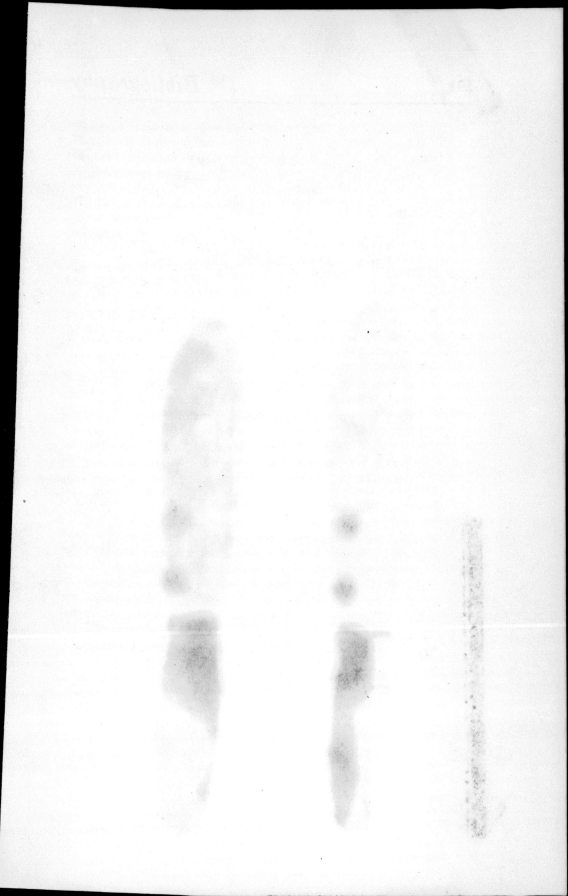